LIPTON'S
AUTOBIOGRAPHY

WITH TWENTY-FOUR ILLUSTRATIONS

DUFFIELD AND GREEN
NEW YORK CITY

Second edition
Especially printed

THE LAST PICTURE OF SIR THOMAS LIPTON, BT.

LIPTON'S AUTOBIOGRAPHY

FOREWORD

I HAD the pleasure of Sir Thomas Lipton's close friendship for many years. Soon after coming to London from Dundee to take up a journalistic appointment in Fleet Street, I was invited by the late Lord Dewar to accompany him to a dinner-party at Osidge, Sir Thomas's beautiful home in north London. Sir Harry Lauder was also of the party, and the four of us—Scotsmen all—formed that night a pact of intimate friendship which was only broken by the death, last year, of the genial, witty, and brilliant Dewar. Now Sir Thomas himself has gone.

Being a journalist, and realizing what a tremendously interesting life Sir Thomas Lipton had lived, and was still living, I repeatedly urged him to publish a book of personal recollections. But for years he remained adamant to all persuasion in this direction. So much so that I ceased to mention the matter further and had rather given up hope of ever seeing a book with Lipton's name on it. However, about two years ago, when Sir Thomas was in the midst of his preparations for his fifth America's Cup Challenge, Lord Dewar himself began to urge the old man to tell the world something of his extraordinary life-story. "Well, Tom," said Lipton, "if you think I should do it, I'll reconsider my decision. But Willie Blackwood must help me with it; I can sell tea and bacon and compete in yacht races, but I am not what could be termed an expert writer!"

And so it was decided that I should assist Sir Thomas in setting forth a plain story of a life which has been altogether without parallel in the realm of international commerce and sport.

I had high hopes of the book being published during the lifetime of Sir Thomas, but for one reason or another I could not get him to come to a definite decision. He seemed to think there was no immediate hurry. "Wait," he recently said to me, "until I *do* win that blooming Cup, and then we'll have something real to crow about!" Cheerful optimism at eighty-one! But that was Sir Thomas all over. Besides, at the back of his wise old head he had the notion that some of his friends might think he was "putting on frills"—a favourite expression of his. And so he passed away, full of years and honour, without seeing his memoirs in the hands of the British public.

For myself, I had intended letting the whole matter drop with his death, but I was asked so frequently to assist with a book about my friend Lipton that I decided to approach Sir Thomas's chief trustees and leave the decision in their hands. Lord Inverforth and Colonel Duncan Neill—both of whom are affectionately referred to in the reminiscences—saw no reason why these should not be published. They knew all about the book when it was being written. For both of them Sir Thomas had an immense respect, and in this he showed his wisdom, for they represent two very fine types of Scottish gentlemen.

W. BLACKWOOD.

CONTENTS

CONTENTS

14

CONTENTS

15

CONTENTS

LIST OF ILLUSTRATIONS

LIST OF ILLUSTRATIONS

LIPTON'S AUTOBIOGRAPHY

CHAPTER I

A good start is half the battle—my mother as a guiding star—my "mixed" nationality—my parents arrive in Glasgow—my father finds work in a cardboard-box-making warehouse—how we lived on twenty-five shillings a week—I discover my ancestry—the Monaghans of Ireland and their disposition for "throuble".

A GOOD start is half the battle. I don't know who originated the phrase, but I do know that nothing more trite or true has been coined in words. I had a good start. For I had a good mother. The best, the bravest-hearted, the noblest mother God ever sent straight from heaven to be one of His angels on earth.

I loved my mother dearly in life and although she has long gone back to the place she came from I can honestly say that no single day elapses without some fragrant memory of my mother coming to me and sweetening the hour of its coming. Her photograph is never far from my hand whether I am on land or on sea: I commune with that dear face many times in every twenty-four hours. Whatever I am, whatever I possess, whatever I have done—all, all is due to the little Irish lady from Clones, in Ulster. She was my guiding star. And by the light of that star I shall steer for the time that yet remains to me.

Those who know me intimately will realize that it would have been impossible for me to begin these chapters reminiscent of a long and amazingly active life without some such reference as I have just made to the memory of my mother. They know—for I have told them over and over again—that she was the most powerful influence in my life as a boy, as a young man, and as a successful merchant springing rather suddenly into what the world calls fame and fortune. I did nothing unless I first consulted her. I relied implicitly on her wisdom and in her unfailing vision. Sooner would I have cut off my right hand than do anything to give her the slightest heart-pang. For me she represented everything that was true, honest, and good. I adored her. Well do I remember as a wee fellow of six or seven putting my arms around her neck and telling her that some day she would ride in a carriage and pair of my providing. For many years before she died she could have had a dozen carriages and pairs had she expressed the very slightest wish for them!

I am invited by hundreds of friends all over the world to write a story of my life—in other words to "look back". As a rule I don't like to look back. I like to look forward. To-morrow has always been for me a more fascinating day than yesterday or the day before that. The yesterdays have gone; the to-morrows remain. Why, here am I, with still another birthday looming invitingly ahead, joyfully looking forward to a certain sporting event in American waters with a relish keener and more enthusiastic than any sensation I have experienced since I opened my first shop in Glasgow. It is occupying all my thoughts and energies and I am keyed up with the hope that the fifth time will, as they say, pay for all. And if not the fifth, well, what about the sixth?

I am often told that I am the world's greatest optimist. Some of the folks who tell me that do so with the suspicion of a sneer. I reply stoutly that I am proud of the distinction. There's something buoyant and healthy in being an optimist. It is because of my optimism that I have gone through life smiling. That I am always in good humour and good fettle. That I refuse to be gloomy about a lot of trouble that will never happen, whether it is next week or next year. Believe me, Dr. Optimist is the finest chap in the "names" directory of any city or country. He and I have been life-long friends and boon companions. Just try a course of his treatment. It will work wonders. And this doctor charges no fees!

While what I have said about my reluctance to look backward is perfectly true in the abstract I am afraid I shall have to indulge in a good deal of retrospective in the course of this volume. Only thus shall I be able to fulfil the request of those friends who assure me that readers enjoy an occasional dip into the past if, in the telling of the tale, there is a smack of combat, a suggestion of difficulties overcome and barriers beaten down, a modest admission of purposes achieved and ambitions accomplished.

Well, writing in all humility, I think I can provide a fairly assorted "blend" of these reminiscent requirements. My only troubles will be in what to tell and what to leave out, where to be frank and where to be guarded, how to keep down the use of the personal pronoun in a narrative which is bound to be almost wholly personal. However, let the proof of the pudding lie in the "preein' o't" as the old Scottish phrase has it!

There has always, I am told, been an air of mystery about my nationality. Both Scotland and Ireland have at different times claimed me as a son. Here are the facts. I was born on the top story of a humble but eminently respectable tenement house in Crown Street, Rutherglen Road, Glasgow. My birth qualifications, therefore, are entirely Scottish. But both my parents were Irish, hailing from the little village of Shannock Green Mills, in the County of Monaghan. The nearest township was Clones, and if you cannot see Shannock Green Mills on your map of Ireland you will certainly see Clones, tucked away in the south-west corner of Monaghan on the borders of Fermanagh almost half-way between

Castleblayney on the east and Enniskillen on the west. So when there is any argument as to my real nationality I come right into the open with the declaration that I am a Scottish-Irishman—or an Irish-Scotsman, according to the leanings of the company I happen to be in at the moment! This pleases the disputants and does me no harm. Mention of this matter reminds me of the days when I used to serve behind the counters of my first stores. I made it my business to study the dialects of both Scotland and Ireland (heaven alone knows how many there are!) so that immediately I detected where a customer was born I could reply in his or her own tongue and thus cement a far closer contact than that merely between shopkeeper and client. I am not exaggerating when I say that in this way I made thousands of customers. Each thought that Thomas Lipton came from his or her own home town and spread the news among their friends. I admitted nothing and denied nothing!

My parents decided to leave Ireland at the time of the great potato famine. The agricultural districts of Ulster, indeed the whole of Ireland, passed through a very bad time round about this period and those emigrants who did not make up their minds to cross the western ocean to the spacious and promising lands of America cast their eyes over a much smaller stretch of water, namely, in the direction of the West of Scotland. The industrial cities and towns of this area were then growing

by leaps and bounds and offering chances of labour
and wages to all who were willing to work. So my
father and mother decided to go to Glasgow. They
sold up their little home, as thousands of Irish
families did at the time, and made their way to
Belfast, crossing over from there to the famous
Broomielaw Quay right in the heart of the great
Scottish city in which I was destined to be born a
few years later.

My father, Thomas Lipton, was a big, broad-
shouldered man, clean of heart and clear-eyed, with
a homely, whiskered face. Among strangers he was
inclined to be shy and backward, but with his own
kith and kin he was genial and boisterous enough
and he had a keen sense of humour which made
him a popular character with all who got to know
him intimately. His ruling passion was his love and
admiration for my mother. If my parents both
regretted the circumstances which severed them for
ever from the Green Isle they loved so deeply, this
fact did not prevent them settling down into good
citizens of the land of their adoption. In a very
short time after landing in Glasgow my father got
a job in a cardboard-box-making warehouse. Later
he became a time-keeper in a paper-mill in McNeill
Street, and this post he held for several years.

I have often heard him say that the highest pay
he ever received as a working man in Glasgow was
from a pound to twenty-five shillings a week. But
in these days, of course, this sum stood for much

more than the same amount would represent to-day. Tens of thousands of families were reared in Scotland forty, fifty and sixty years ago—and respectably reared, moreover—on weekly incomes which to-day would mean absolute poverty and privation. At the time of which I write, and for many years afterwards, there were good men in the towns and villages of Scotland who brought up large families on wages which never exceeded those of my father and who contrived to send one, at least, of their sons to the University. And there were no Carnegie scholarships in these days either!

While my parents took very kindly to the new life in the great city of Glasgow their thoughts often wandered back to Ireland, and amongst my earliest recollections are of them sitting of an evening over the fireside in our house in Crown Street and recalling the scenes and incidents of their childhood and young married days at Shannock Green Mills. I loved to hear them speak of the folks "at home" and to listen to stories of the Liptons and the other warm-hearted, jovial people of Shannock Green Mills and the surrounding district. These Liptons, according to my father and mother, were a well-known family and much respected in Monaghan. They seem never to have achieved individual fame or prominence, but they were a lively, happy, rollicking lot, always ready for a joke, or a "barney" or even a fight—a typical Irish family.

Some people, I have noticed, spend half their

lives boasting of their illustrious ancestors. They forget that these ancestors are like the potato—the best part of them is underground! I often wonder what some of these ancestors would think if they could come back and see some of their descendants to-day. I am afraid the "ghosts" would take one quick look, draw a long breath, and hurry back to the shades immediately. It is not what a man's grandfather was that counts to-day, or even what his father was. The only thing that matters is what a man has made of his own life. In America they don't worry overmuch about ancestors—they are all too busy making their own ancestry, and I like them for it! But while saying all this and most thoroughly believing it, I was rather interested recently to come across a most fascinating book entitled "Monaghan in the Eighteenth Century".

The author of this volume, Dr. Denis Carolin Rushe, has been at some pains to find out all that he can about the Lipton family. His investigations carry him as far back as two hundred years ago and even in these days, he says, the Liptons were not unknown in the annals of the county in which they belonged. They were, in fact, "broths of boys", full of fun and frivolity, laughter and jollity, and took an active part in the politics and "ploys" of that interesting period. The "Lipton Ones" (as they were called in the local parlance of the times) were usually mixed up in all the high jinks that took place in and around Clones. Dr. Rushe tells many

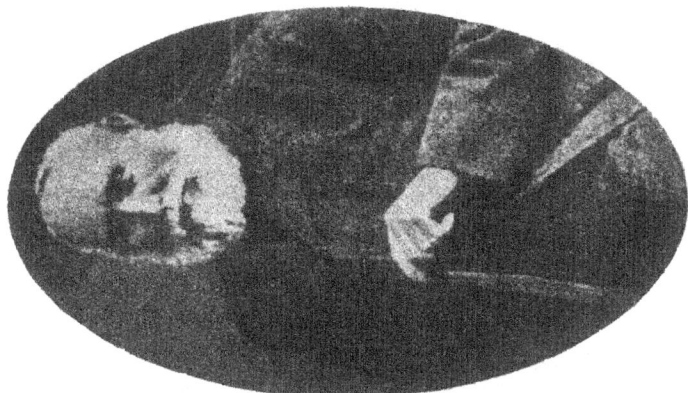

HIS FATHER

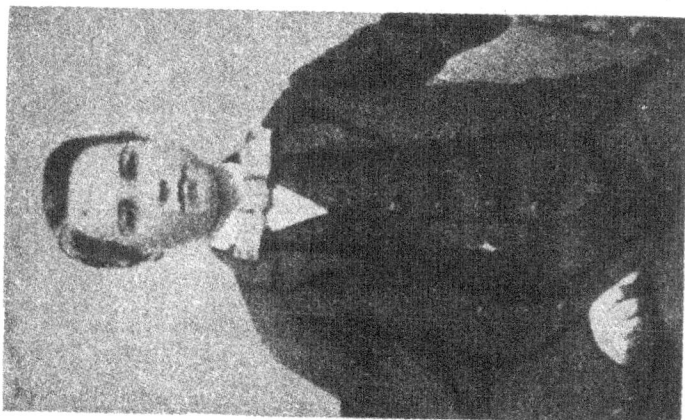

THOMAS LIPTON AT THE
AGE OF 12

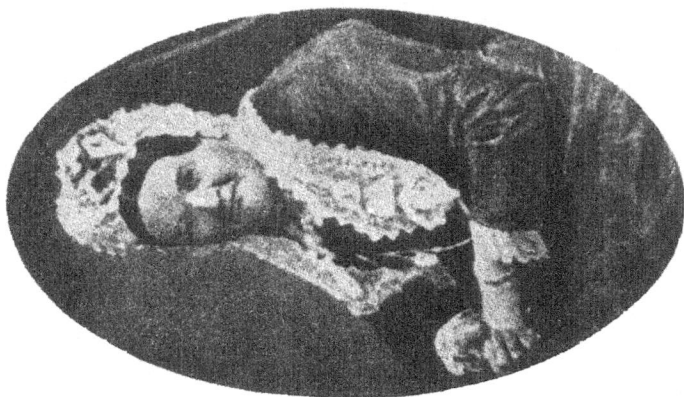

HIS MOTHER

amusing stories of their spirited adventures and escapades and his book makes delightful reading.

When in 1770, for example, an elopement caused a great sensation in the district, the "Lipton Ones" were well in the picture. In that year, Elizabeth Graham, the daughter of a Scottish farmer who had settled in Kilmore, was evidently the reigning beauty of the locality. All the young bloods worshipped at her shrine, but the lad who found most favour in her eyes was a farmer named Nicholls. Parental objections on the part of the Graham family did not allow the course of true love to run smoothly and Nicholls at last decided to elope with the girl. To ensure that his plans should be crowned with success what was more natural than that he should enlist the aid of his dashing cousins, the Lipton boys of Shannock Green Mills? The request, and the prospect it held out, was very much to their taste. A council of war was called. Direct action was decided upon. The Graham "fastness" was raided next night and the girl carried off and handed over to her lover.

There was a terrible uproar in the district. Old Graham did not take the outrage calmly, but gathered his friends and retainers together, armed them to the teeth, and set out to wreak vengeance and recover his beloved daughter. How many heads were broken in the skirmishes which ensued the author of "Monaghan in the Eighteenth Century" does not say, but there was a legal sequel, for the Lipton Ones and their allies were duly arrested and made their appearance at the next Assizes where they were charged "with forcibly carrying away one Elizabeth Graham". Those indicted were George Nicholls, William Lipton, Robert Lipton, John Lipton, William Coine, William Mahaffy, Michael M'Caffrey, and Hugh Maguire. The Graham faction were determined to have the culprits hanged to the last man, for in these days the crime of carrying off a woman was a capital offence, and they employed the best barristers in Ireland to assist them in their efforts. But the case collapsed suddenly when Elizabeth Graham went into the witness-box and smilingly stated that she loved George Nicholls and had gone away with him of her own free-will, adding that the "Lipton Ones" had simply come on the scene to wish her God-speed. The prosecution had reckoned without the girl, as often happens in such cases!

But my ancestors seem to have had a special liking for "throuble" of this description. Mr. Rushe points out that some years before the affair of the Graham elopement there had been a very bitter dispute between landlords and tenants in Monaghan. The side of the farmers was valiantly championed by three of the Liptons of Shannock Green Mills and this trio, doubtless among other misdeeds, joyfully accepted an opportunity one evening to set about a bailiff and his assistant and give them a thorough good hiding. There is something about the word "bailiff" which for centuries has acted as a red rag to a bull so far as both Irishmen and Scotsmen are concerned, and even at this day I cannot find it in my heart to blame these ancient Liptons for their action. At all events they were arrested and tried at Enniskillen in 1767. I am glad to read that they were acquitted for good and sound reason that "no Fermanagh jury could bring itself to convict a Lipton"! In a record of this particular trial which has been preserved and now brought to light by the researches of Mr. Carolin Rushe, it would appear that judge and jury lunched particularly well. The clerk of the court did not limit himself in these days to a cold, legal record of the proceedings, otherwise we would not have had the amazing statement that "after the jury returned from their midday meal some of them were drunk, others pretty drunk and others, again, damned drunk!" Who shall say that these were not "spacious days"?

CHAPTER II

Boyhood days in Glasgow—I represent the family in Church on Sunday morning—my parents open a wee shop and embark upon the provision trade—a wheelbarrow to the docks for weekly supplies—schooldays and street battles—from which I emerge a sorry spectacle—an early passion for sailing craft—I sail my first Shamrock at the tender age of eleven—home influences are best.

CROWN STREET, Glasgow, where I was born and spent my early years, still stands, and is pretty well the same thoroughfare as it was when it was my home. Not a very long street, it partakes of the character of thousands of other Scottish city thoroughfares in which the respectable working classes have their "tenement" dwelling-places. A tenement, perhaps I should explain, is a building of three or four or more stories sub-divided into different small houses. The latter may consist of two or three or four rooms, seldom more, although in the better-class districts of Glasgow I have known tenements which provide "flats" of six and seven rooms.

The Lipton family occupied four rooms on the top story and the rent, if I recollect rightly, was twelve pounds, ten shillings a year with the municipal taxes in addition. By no stretch of imagination could our house be termed elegant or artistic, but scrupulously clean and comfortable it was. My mother saw to it that it was kept, as the saying has it, like "a new pin"; you could have eaten your food off the floor and certainly you could have seen your face reflected in the highly-polished kitchen-"grate", or fireplace. Like the majority of Glasgow housewives, she took a tremendous interest in her humble home and no effort was too much to keep it spick and span. I well remember the scoldings I used to receive if ever I dared to come over the outside door without wiping my feet on the mat. Even as a very small boy I was proud of my home and proud of Crown Street—particularly as it was "near the Blazes"! Glasgow folk all over the world will know at once what the phrase means. "Dixon's Blazes" has been the name universally bestowed for the past hundred years on the great blast furnaces which still stand at the top of Crown Street and remain to this day an object of constant admiration and fascination to thousands of Glasgow children.

Although I did not know it at the time, Crown Street had other claims to fame in addition to being "near the Blazes", for, many years before my advent there, it had been the temporary home of Robert Pollock, the brilliant young Scottish poet, author of "The Course of Time", during his studies at Glasgow University. About the same time, too, I believe that James Naysmith, the inventor of the steam hammer, often walked up and down its grimy

C

pavements while serving part of his apprenticeship at Dixon's Blast Furnaces. These facts I learned in after years and they added to my love and veneration for the old street which was my first home and in which I spent so many happy days.

Let me recall, too, that in my own boyhood's time at Crown Street there lived, next door to the house in which I was born, two quiet working men who were destined to play a very big part in modern industrial development. Almost every evening and certainly every Saturday afternoon these brothers retired to a wash-house at the back of the tenement, locked themselves in and proceeded to conduct experiments of a peculiarly foul-smelling description. From the crevices in the door and window emerged smoke and fumes of, as it appeared to my wondering eyes, different colours and density. The neighbours were not slow to complain of the terrible, throat-catching effluvium which found its way into their homes and I can remember the profound impression that was caused upon me by an old, Highland wife proclaiming, from the house-tops, as it were, the curse that would befall the street if the authorities did not step in and stop these "warlocks and their devil's brew"! The young experimenters were none other than Robert and James Dick, the inventors of gutta-percha and the founders of the world-famous firm of R. & J. Dick.

In spite of the awful smells and the air of

mystery which hung about that little outhouse in Crown Street, Glasgow—or, more probably, because of them—I was fascinated beyond measure by the two quiet, purposeful brothers and it was a joyful moment when they asked me into the shed one Saturday afternoon and invited me to assist them in their work. Naturally their plant was of the most primitive order—an old copper or two for boiling the gutta and an ancient printing-press which they used for squeezing the prepared solution down to the necessary thickness for soling boots and shoes. My task was to scrape the coppers free from the "gutty" after it had been heated. My reward was the scrapings which I could have taken away with me had I been inclined, but I was so enthusiastic about the business of rubber-sole making that generally I insisted on the scrapings going back into the next "brew"! People all over the world have been much interested when I have told them that I was "closely associated with the rubber industry in its very earliest days". Robert and James Dick have long since gone to their fathers. They achieved great and deserved success and their names will live for a very long time in the industrial history of Scotland and of the world.

The Lipton household about this time consisted of my father and mother, my brother John and my sister Margaret. There had been two other brothers who had died in infancy. All those who preceded me were of delicate constitution. John lived until he was nineteen. He was frail in body but full of grit and ambition. He was determined to be a doctor and on leaving school he worked in a chemist's shop in Virginia Street. Out of his scanty pay he managed to save enough to enter for classes at Glasgow University and had it been God's will to spare him I have no doubt he would have made a name for himself. His death was a sad blow to our father and mother and to me also who regarded Big Brother John with something akin to hero-worship. My sister Margaret, or Maggie as we called her at home, lived for several years after John's death, but she likewise was taken away in early womanhood. Happily for my father and mother, I seem to have been made of sterner stuff than the other members of the family. Except for one brief period when something went wrong with my eyesight and I had to make a series of much-dreaded visits to the old Glasgow Eye Hospital in Charlotte Street, I was rarely ill and went on to develop a strong and hardy constitution. Why this should have been so and why I should have gone through life without a real day's illness I have always been at a loss to understand. I can only put it down to the inscrutable workings of Providence.

Up till the time I left Glasgow to make my head-quarters in London I often used to visit Crown Street merely to glance up at the old windows and to recall, on the spot, so to speak, the scenes and haunts of my poor but happy boyhood.

Pondering on these early days I sometimes find myself wondering how my mother succeeded in keeping a comfortable roof above our heads, feeding us and clothing us, on the scanty wages earned by my father. Even allowing that money went farther in these days than it does now it has always been a mystery to me. We had an abundance of good food, in which porridge and Scotch broth, potato soup, home-baked scones and oatcakes played an important part. My mother was clever with her needle and she made practically all my clothes. She was never idle from morning till night. And I cannot recall her without a smile on her face and a cheery word on her tongue.

She taught me to hold my head high and to have ideals in life. Honesty, courage and truthfulness were her chief tenets in the philosophy of life; she never tired of impressing these essentials on my young mind. Religion, too, played a strong part in the Lipton household. My mother had the ingrained conviction that no matter what might befall her and her dear ones she and they need fear nothing so long as they feared God.

Regularly every Sabbath we went to the Hutchesontown Established Church of Scotland in Cleland Street. I liked going to church for one thing particularly and that was to see the respect in which my parents were held by the minister and

37

other members of the congregation. And when there was any special preacher, such as the famous Reverend Norman McLeod, the chaplain to Queen Victoria, due to occupy our pulpit, seats were reserved for us and we were admitted to the church by a side door so as to escape the crowd which always turns up at a Scottish church when a "good preacher" is announced. On occasions like these my breast swelled with pride to think that I was a Lipton and because "my people" were entitled to such a privilege and honour.

On one never-to-be-forgotten Sunday morning I was sent to church alone—"to represent the family", as my mother said on giving me my final brush-down and putting my penny for the plate in my hand. I could not have been more than six or seven years old. The elder at the door conducted me to a seat directly facing the minister, a good, but stern-faced Scottish divine of the old school who thundered forth a powerful and eloquent sermon from the text, "Am I my brother's keeper—" I say "powerful and eloquent" because I have no doubt whatever that the sermon was all this and more. The only thing I remember about it, apart from the text, was that the preacher kept glaring at me most of the time, making me more and more fidgety and self-conscious as he proceeded. Finally, after an overwhelming torrent of words the good man in the pulpit pointed straight at me, as I thought, and repeated the question three times, "Am

I my brother's keeper?" With the repetition of the momentous query for the third time his blazing eyes caught my own. Terrified, I thought it was absolutely necessary for me to reply, so I shouted out at the pitch of my voice: "Yes, sir!" Preacher and congregation were alike dumbfounded and soon a titter went round the church which was with difficulty repressed, as the police court reporters say. I remember that I was painfully conscious of having, as I thought, "disgraced the Lipton family" and ran, weeping, all the way home.

It was an eventful day in our family history when my father and mother decided to embark upon a new method of gaining a livelihood. There was a tiny, wee shop—with three steps down from the street level—to let at 13 Crown Street and this they decided to lease and start in the retail provision trade.

They had no experience of shopkeeping, but, they argued, people had to eat to live and why shouldn't they start a small shop from which they could sell to their neighbours the wherewithal of their daily meals. The decision to open this shop was not come to suddenly; many anxious and prayerful hours were spent by my father and mother discussing ways and means, difficulties and prospects. They had only a few pounds saved up and failure would have meant disaster. But they had faith and energy and determination; all they desired was a bare living and the thought of "success"—in the ordinary sense of the word—and money-making never entered into their calculations.

So the little shop was taken. It was so small that half a dozen people would have had to jostle to get inside it at the same time. But the place itself was spotlessly clean and the stock-in-trade was the same. Ham, butter and eggs were the main items of the latter. My mother had arranged with an old friend in Clones, one James McAviney, a peasant farmer, to send over every week a supply of hams, butter and eggs. It was my duty to take a wheelbarrow every Monday to the Irish steamer and bring back to the shop the total week's supplies. For this job of work my mother paid me twopence —my first weekly earnings in commerce.

I took an intense interest in my parents' new venture. It was moderately prosperous from the first. The customers could be sure of sound food at a reasonable price, but what was even more important they were served by transparently honest people whom they had known for years in the district in which the shop was situated. In addition to acting as very youthful porter and bringing the weekly supplies to Crown Street from the Irish steamer shed at the Broomielaw, I helped my father in keeping the shop tidy, in polishing the counter and the window—there was but one and a small one at that—and running messages for my mother and delivering goods to customers. That there must have been some latent ideas in my head about shopkeeping even in these days seems to be proved by a remark made to my father one morning after I had seen him serve a customer with half a dozen eggs. I asked him: "Why don't you let mother serve the eggs, dad? You see mother's hands are much smaller than yours and the eggs would look much bigger in her hands than they do in yours?" For many years afterwards I was often chaffed regarding this suggestion, which was held to be a wise and precocious notion for a small boy.

Of my school days I have little to say. My mother gave very anxious thoughts to the problem of my education. She could not afford to send me to any expensive school. But there was no need to, for there were in Glasgow in those days, as there is to-day, an abundance of splendid schools in which a boy or girl could get a very thorough grounding, if not a very lengthy one, in the rudiments of practical education. Scotland has always been famous for its schools and schooling and it is but stating a commonly acknowledged fact to assert that this has had much to do with the pre-eminence of the Scottish race the wide world over.

I was sent first to St. Andrew's Parish School, facing Glasgow Green. The headmaster was one, Lochhead, of whose scholarship and faculties for bringing out the best that was in a boy my mother had frequently heard. My school-fees were three-pence a week, the money being paid over to the headmaster every Monday morning. Mr.

Lochhead was a Scottish dominie of the old type, wise, solemn and severe, but with a kindly disposition peeping out, unwillingly almost, in many of his actions. He earned the unbounded respect of the majority of his pupils. The wilder spirits amongst them might try a "trick or two" with him now and then, but they only did it once! I cannot say that I was either a favourite or a very diligent pupil at St. Andrew's. Indeed, my mother came to the conclusion that I was not making sufficient progress under Mr. Lochhead and she moved me to another school for a short period. Here, however, the results were definitely not what my mother had hoped for, and back again I was dispatched to St. Andrew's, where I remained until the close of my school career. Mr. Lochhead lived to a ripe old age and I may be pardoned for saying that throughout the latter years of his life he was very proud of his old pupil, Tommy Lipton.

By the time I had entered my "teens" I had grown into a big, strong lad with my fair share of mischief and devilment. I was always ready for any fun or frolic that happened to be going on. There were lots of lads of my own age in Crown Street and round about the district and I was a ringleader in all manner of "ploys" and escapades and adventures. Mere high spirits were responsible for us forming ourselves into what we called the "Crown Street Clan" and going forth to find what excitement we could in attacking combinations of

LIPTON'S FIRST SHOP IN STOBCROSS STREET, GLASGOW

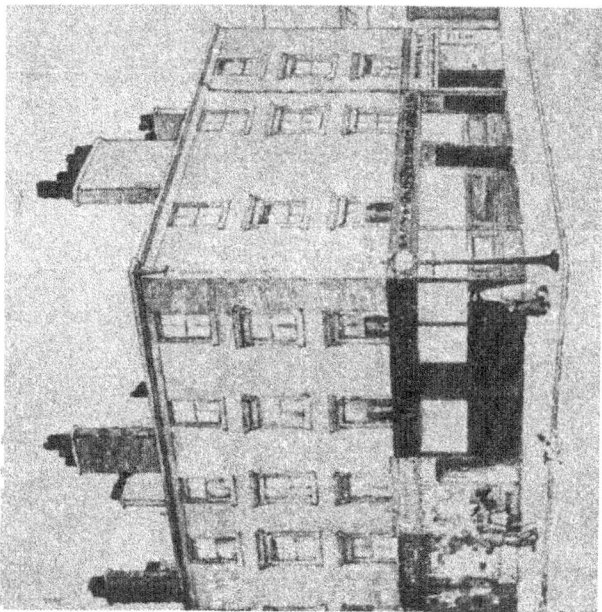

THE BIRTHPLACE OF THOMAS JOHNSTONE LIPTON

boys from other quarters of the town. Sometimes we lost and sometimes we won. But you may depend upon it that we thoroughly enjoyed ourselves.

As a leader in these street battles I had learned how to use my fists. In my young days in Glasgow any boy who did not know how to defend himself when called upon was regarded by his pals as a "fushionless craitur". Generally a boy had to go "through it" before he was admitted a member of any local gang and by his conduct and bearing in a series of fistic encounters was his reputation made or marred. How well do I remember my first real fight! "Wullie" was the son of a butcher and he was known and hated as the Bully of Crown Street. He was a great hulking lout of a boy and we smaller fellows had to pay him tribute at every game of marbles we played. One day, however, my young blood got the better of me and I flatly refused to part with some of the "bools" I had won in fair contest. He threatened me and although I was much younger than he was, I thereupon challenged him to fight. Most of my comrades urged me to withdraw, telling me point blank that "Wullie" would kill me. Others urged me to put a stop, once and for all—if I were able that is to say—to the domination of the hated bully. "A fight! A fight!" The words ran through our street like wildfire. Off we went, principals and supporters, to a court at the back of Crown Street where

43

there was little chance of the combat being over-looked or interfered with.

These were the days when the pugilistic encounters between Heenan and Sayers, the other famous English and American champions, had captured the imagination of every mother's son on both sides of the Atlantic. Everything was done according to rule. The combatants retired each into his corner and proceeded to strip to the waist. In the meantime, seconds were appointed, also a referee and a timekeeper—the latter being the only youth in the whole crowd who could produce a watch. In fact, the preliminaries to the fight could not have been more scientifically conducted had they been in charge of Jack Dempsey himself or the Chairman of the National Sporting Club. "Time" was duly called and at it we went, hammer and tongs. Round after round I came up for my medicine. But I gave "Wullie" a good deal more than he bargained for. The upshot of it all was that I received a severe beating, my seconds throw-ing in the towel at the end of the fifth or sixth round. Far from lording his success over me and my companions, I must hand it to "Wullie" that he left us alone for the future. As a result of my fight with the bully, my stock soared high among all the boys of the district. My mother was much distressed when she learned that I had been fighting, but I fancied I saw a merry twinkle in my father's eye when I told him that I had stood up for so many rounds against "Wullie" Ross, the butcher's boy.

Another adventure I had at this time I can recall as clearly as if it had happened yesterday. The Crown Street boys had much annoyed a certain "peeler"—as we used to call a policeman—by refusing to desist from playing some of our noisy games in the centre of the thoroughfare. He swore to get even with us and particularly that "young varmint, Tommy Lipton". Suddenly, in the middle of a game, our enemy appeared as if from nowhere. With his coat-tails flying and holding his high hat with one hand and gripping his baton in the other, he charged down on our gang. It was obvious from the start that he intended to collar me. I ran as hard as my legs would carry me, visions of the birch-rod flaming in my mind, and it was only by doubling up a "through-going close" that I was able, for the time being, to get away from the limb of the law. At the top of the close was a place known as Kerr's Byre (a byre in Scotland is a build-ing in which cows are housed) and in my anxiety to escape from the pursuing peeler, I jumped on to a rubbish-heap in order to scale a wall on the other side of which was a road to safety. Alas, the "mound" was nothing like so solid as I had expected it to be and down I sank to my armpits in mud and "glaur". To add to my discomfiture, the officer came up but, instead of arresting me, he started to laugh and jeer at my calamity. "Serves ye right, me lad!" he said, and left me to wriggle my way out of the filthy heap the best way I could.

Making my way to a public pump in Govan Street—an object of misery to myself and amusement to others—I there did my utmost to purify myself. My misfortune awakened the compassion of an old cobbler's wife who took me into the little kitchen behind her husband's shop, stripped off my clothes, rolled me in a blanket and put me to bed. Then she washed and dried my clothes so that, two hours later, I was able to present myself at home with little outward appearance of the disaster which had overtaken me.

Looking back on these days now I come to the conclusion that in spite of the schoolboy pranks and the exciting hours as leader of the Crown Street Clan, my happiest days were spent by the riverside. As business in the little shop increased my visits with my wheelbarrow to the Irish steamer became more and more frequent. Some days the ship would be late and at other times I had to wait quite a long while until my little share of the big cargo was hoisted on to the quay. These periods of waiting I utilized to the full by wandering all over the wharves and docks studying the different steamers and craft of all kinds using the wonderful, man-made river of Clyde. I spoke to sailors, stevedores, dock-labourers, engineers. My favourite question was "Where has *your* ship come from?" In this way did I learn more geography than I ever picked up at school, for I bought a cheap map of the world and found immense delight in tracing the voyages of the various ships—this one from China, that from Calcutta, the next from far Peru.

The American passenger boats always held my unbounded admiration. They were mere cockle-shells compared to the magnificent liners which now carry me to and from America several times a year, but to my boyhood's eye they were immense galleons linking Scotland with the El Dorados of the West and of which everybody was now beginning to speak with almost bated breath. One afternoon I saw a party of emigrants boarding a steamer bound for New York. How I wished I could have made one of the party! New York, at that time, was becoming a magic name for ambitious youth the world over and secretly I determined that some day I would see the great city myself, and perhaps even penetrate the mysteries of the Golden West!

In this way I developed a passion for ships and shipping and everything connected with the ocean, from the greatest steamers that sailed the seas down to the little boats and sailing craft thronging the waters of the Clyde below and above the old Broomielaw Bridge. This passion has never left me and is, indeed, stronger in my breast to-day than ever it was. By the time I was eleven years old I could ply a pair of oars or single-scull a coble and very soon afterwards sail a lugsail boat with the best of the Clydeside watermen. It is true that I did not get many chances of sailing, but every now and then, when I had saved up a few coppers, I would hire a "cat-boat" and indulge my hobby to the full.

My "debut" as a yachtsman took place when I was about eleven years old! As a matter of fact, I founded a Yacht Club and was its first commodore! It came about in this way. So keen was I on ships and yachts that I resolved to build a model with my own hands. From the massive lid of an old wooden chest I carved, with infinite labour, and by the use of an old "gully" knife, the hull of a boat to which I afterwards added a mast and bowsprit with rigging. The sails I made of strong paper. When all was shipshape I carried this much-treasured craft to a field known as the High Green, not far from Crown Street. In this field were several huge holes, relics of old brickmaking operations, which had become filled up with muddy water, and on the largest of these "ponds" I launched my first yacht! Can you fancy what her name was? The *Shamrock*! Joy of joys! Not only did she float, and on an even keel, but she sailed across the pond like a thing of life at the first time of asking. Not once in all the crowded years which have come and gone since then have I ever recaptured the thrill of the launch and the first "race" of the original *Shamrock*.

My companions quickly followed me in this new

and absorbing game. They, too, built boats after the fashion of my own and soon yacht-racing on the water-holes of the High Green became the order of the day. Boat was matched against boat. Improvements in the build and rig were constantly tried out. Challenges were thrown down and accepted. The stakes were generally a certain number of "bools" and these were deposited before the race in the "bannet" of Commodore Tommy Lipton. As a founder of the new sport and of the "club" my word in all matters affecting the races was accepted as absolute. In all the important races I acted as referee unless, of course, the *Shamrock* was a competitor. I won many races and lost a few. And I think I can say with all truth that it was on the muddy banks of the clay-holes in High Green that I learned one of the greatest lessons in life—how to win with pleasure and lose with a smile.

Childhood, after all, is the one really blissful period in existence. It matters not whether the bairn be born of low estate or cradled in the lap of luxury; there is something in the early years that has little to do with environment but which insists on every child having its fair share of a certain type of happiness. I would go farther and assert that the children of the very poor are often far happier than those of the rich. My old friend, Andrew Carnegie, himself a child of the people, once wisely said: "I pity the

49

sons and daughters of rich men who are attended by governesses and servants. They do not know what they have missed. They have fathers and mothers—very kind fathers and mothers too—and they think they enjoy the sweetness of those blessings to the full, but this they cannot do. For the poor boy who has in his father his constant companion, tutor and model, and in his mother—holy name—his nurse, teacher, guardian angel, saint, all in one, has a richer and more precious fortune than any rich man's son can possibly know and compared with which all other fortunes count as little." With every word of this I most thoroughly agree!

Although as a boy I was very poor, I was rich in the possession of parents whose home influence was always of the best. Home is the laboratory of character, the one spot where early and lasting impressions are formed for good or ill. True, I had to make the streets, and the docks, and the old brickyard ponds my playgrounds, but they yielded me a much wider area for fun and frolic, for roving in the lands of imaginary adventure and make-believe so dear to the heart of a boy, than ever I could have obtained in the most palatial nursery of the biggest castle in Scotland. They gave me, too, a more liberal education in the give-and-take, the rough-and-tumble of life than I could have got as a high school graduate. By mixing freely with other children I early came to a knowledge of human nature and the necessity of keeping my own end up. We are told that the race is "neither to the swift nor the battle to the strong". There may be exceptions to the general rule; in my case it was borne in upon me very early that the "race" is usually won by both the swift *and* the strong!

CHAPTER III

My first job at the age of nine—and farewell to school-days—the joy of my first week's pay—a fight and a reprimand—we plan to surprise "Auld Specky"—and I change my job—life as a cabin-boy—my first week's notice.

I SEEM to have had a dash of both qualities. For without asking my parents' permission I left school and took my first job. Business had been very bad in the wee shop for some months. Profits were scarcely sufficient to keep the household going in the bare necessities. The few sovereigns my father and mother had been able to save when trade was fair were gradually eaten up and there came a time when it was very doubtful if the shop could continue to pay its way. I was only between nine and ten years of age, but I realized how tight was the corner in which the Lipton family now found themselves. My heart ached to see my father looking sad and worried, and my mother, with her usual courage, pretending that she wasn't. I must do something to help them, I told myself. Taking my school-bag with me, I left the house one dismal November morning in 1860. But I did not go to school. Wandering round the city I found myself in Glassford Street, and my eye was suddenly attracted to the familiar notice, "Boy Wanted:

Apply Within", stuck up in the window of a shop occupied, as the name-plate above the door indicated, by "A. & W. Kennedy, Stationers". Without a second's hesitation I walked into the shop and asked "if the job"—nodding in the direction of the window—"had been filled". The manager replied that it hadn't and gave me a rapid glance up and down. "You can start at once," was all that he said, adding as a sort of afterthought: "Your wages will be half-a-crown a week!" Five minutes afterwards I was cleaning that window!

At the end of the day's work I ran all the way home to impart the good news to my father and mother. My father smiled his droll smile, but my mother started to weep, a proceeding which I could not understand at the time, for I was hoping she would be overjoyed at my pluck and success. At first she wanted me to give up the job and return to school, but this I would not listen to. The first day of independence and freedom had whetted my appetite; I was full of enthusiasm and self-confidence—certain that I was on the high-road to fame and fortune. To abandon the post I had been so lucky to secure was unthinkable. Besides, I argued, I would be earning money and helping to keep myself. At the end my parents capitulated, and I went to bed that night the proudest little chap in Glesca Toon.

School inspectors were then unknown. There was no Education Authority to interfere with any lad who wished to work—or was driven out to work by necessity—no matter how young he might be, and so I became one of those curious little bundles of humanity that marked the pre-School Board era —half-boy, half-man. The hours I was called upon to work were long and the labour was hard for a child of ten, but my employers were decent, honest Glasgow tradesmen, and I served them with a willing, joyful heart. When, at the end of my first week, I received the shining half-crown that was my reward for six days of such work as your modern boy would most certainly refuse to tackle, I felt that the wide world was mine for the taking. Tightly clenching the half-crown in my right hand and keeping that same hand deep hidden in my trouser pocket, I hurried to the wee shop in Crown Street and proudly placed my wages in my mother's "lap". You can imagine for yourself our combined emotions.

Some few years ago, as Honorary Colonel of the Sixth Highland Light Infantry, with a thousand of the finest men in the world marching behind me, I rode past that same shop in Glassford Street in which I started work. I had to swallow hard and set my chin. Each beat of the big drum brought clearer to my memory the days when the salesman in the shop stamped his heel on the floor, and, in obedience to the summons, I used to come running up from the basement, to be dispatched upon some errand. I recalled, too, how often in the old days,

COMING FROM LIPTON

GOING TO LIPTON

ONE OF THE EARLIEST LIPTON ADVERTISEMENTS WHICH WERE DISPLAYED IN THE WINDOWS OF HIS SHOPS. THESE CRUDE BUT LAUGHABLE CARTOONS WERE ALTERED WEEK' BY WEEK AND PEOPLE FLOCKED FROM ALL OVER GLASGOW TO SEE THEM

at the sound of martial music, I had stolen out of the old shop, undetected, to see a regiment of soldiers go past and listen to the skirl of the pipes. And now I was a colonel myself in brave, red uniform and riding a prancing horse! Could I ever in my wildest dreams have conceived of such a metamorphosis?

During the next few years I plunged pretty deeply into the rush and turmoil of industrial life in the West Country, as Glasgow and the surrounding district is known all over Scotland. Tempted by a rise in wages from half-a-crown to four shillings a week, I left the Kennedys and went to Messrs. Tillie & Henderson, then, as now, trading at 39 Miller Street, and then, as they still are, the largest firm of shirt-makers in Glasgow. I believe they claim to make more shirts than any other firm in the world. My job here was the singularly dull and uninspiring task of cutting cloth patterns and gumming them into the sample books carried by travellers. But there were occasional interludes to vary the monotony. For instance, I had a terrific fight with another boy in the pattern department one day. I did not know that the head of the firm, Mr. Henderson, an elderly Scot of stern countenance, and a martinet to business application on the part of his staff, had an office on the second floor from which he could look down, unseen, on the workers below. Unfortunately for me he was a spectator of this combat in which I was an easy victor, the other boy retiring from the fray with a bleeding nose and a black eye. The boss promptly sent for me and upbraided me for "my disgraceful conduct in business hours".

"What explanation have you to offer?" he asked.

"I hit him, sir," I answered, "because he cut the toorie aff ma bonnet."

"That does not justify you making a fellow-worker's nose bleed," said my angry chief.

"Well, I will admit I can get a new bonnet and he canna' get a new nose!" I answered.

After I had been at Tillie & Henderson's for a month or two I thought I was entitled to a rise in my pay. So I wrote out an application asking for an extra shilling a week. This I slipped in amongst the firm's letters one morning. Convinced that my whole future lay in how this request would be answered I anxiously waited the result. At the end of a day or two I received a pencilled note from the cashier. All it contained was the following: "You are getting as much as you are worth and you are in a devil of a hurry asking for a rise!"

Time has a curious way of ringing the changes, however. The next letter to reach me from this same firm was not written until many years later. As a matter of fact I received it in 1915, as I was about to leave England with one of my Red Cross parties on my steam yacht *Erin*, to Salonica— *en route* for Serbia.

Signed by D. A. Sinclair, chairman of the firm,
the letter ran as follows:

Dear Sir Thomas,

A young lady friend whom I have known
for many years is going out to Serbia as a
V.A.D. nurse in your next Red Cross party,
and if at any time you find you can render
her any little attention I should be greatly
obliged as she is a personal friend of my wife
and daughters.

On receipt of this I at once told my secretary
to ring up the writer on the telephone. I then went
to the phone myself and promised to do all I could
for the young lady.

I next asked Mr. Sinclair: "Are you the same
Mr. Sinclair who worked in Tillie & Henderson's
when I was there as a lad, or was it your father?"
And he replied: "It was I."

"Why," I said, "I remember you well, although
you were much higher up than I was—you wore a
frock coat!"

I then went on to say: "What a contrast this
letter is from the last one I received from your firm!
When I got that last letter I was working for 4/- a
week and had just asked for a shilling rise, and the
only reply I got was a pencilled scrap of paper
from the cashier saying 'I was getting as much as
I was worth and was in a devil of a hurry asking
for a rise'. And now the chairman writes to ask

me to look after a friend who is going out with the party of doctors, nurses and orderlies I am taking with me on my hospital ship, *Erin*, to Salonica! A bit of a change in the tune of the two letters, eh?"

Poor Mr. Sinclair hesitated and appeared to be embarrassed. Then he heard me laughing at the end of the telephone and realized that I was only pulling his leg. He became from then onwards one of my greatest friends.

The curt refusal of my application for a rise in wages discontented me at Tillie & Henderson's, and although I stayed on for a period I lost all my enthusiasm for the dreary task of cutting out shirt-patterns. During the few months I remained in their employment I attended a night-school in Rutherglen Road.

The master of my class at this night-school was a crusty, ill-tempered old crank, who wore big-rimmed, blue spectacles and was known to everybody in the district as "Auld Specky". That he was sound enough in the fundamentals of his profession I have no doubt and must admit that I made considerable progress under his tuition. But the man did not seem to have the slightest atom of humanity in his make-up; he was a fish-blooded tyrant of whom Dickens would have made a character. "Specky" was a whole-hearted adherent of the Biblical theory about sparing the rod and spoiling the child. Heavens! How he must have loved us! During school hours we even trembled when he looked at us and few of the pupils escaped condign punishment from time to time.

It is not, therefore, to be wondered at that several of his juvenile victims, immediately their school periods were over, laid plans for getting "a bit of their own back". With the assistance of two other erstwhile scholars who had often felt the weight of the master's "tawse" I paid a surprise visit to the school at an hour when we knew "Specky" would be alone. Having tied the doorhandle firmly with rope so that he could not get out, we plugged the keyhole with an evil-smelling substance known in these days as "Diel's Fodder", which we had purchased from a Crown Street druggist's shop. This awful compound we then lighted. By the aid of pipe-shanks we blew the fumes into the school-room. "Specky's" rage and mortification and utter discomfort we beheld gloatingly from one of the windows and it was not until the wretched dominie was nearly suffocated that we freed the door and allowed him to make his escape.

Ultimately I left Tillie & Henderson's. Whether it was that I had lost heart over the "rise" that didn't materialize, or simply craved for a change, I cannot now recall. Perhaps it was that at the back of my mind there was a hankering to see a bit more of the great world. I was never happier, as I have told, than when in the atmosphere of ships, sailors, boats and the waterside generally. By a lucky chance I heard one day that there was an opening for a cabin-boy on one of the Burns Liners regularly plying between the Broomielaw and Belfast. Dreading that I might be too late I hurried along to the steamer offices, applied for the job—and got it. Wages—eight shillings a week and my keep on board. A millionaire's rise! Feeling six inches taller and twice as broad, I went home and broke the news to my mother.

Naturally, she did not like the idea of so small a boy leaving the roof-tree but both she and my father realized that the change meant a big step-up for me.

My work as a cabin-boy on a small cross-channel steamer was hard and endless; there is no starting hour or closing time on a passenger ship making nightly trips over a particularly rough stretch of water. Day merges into night, and night into day, in a remorseless sort of continuity. It is work, work, all the time until the eyes become heavy and the feet weary. Yet I can honestly say that I was completely enthralled, both night and day. I took an endless delight in the ship herself; in the engines which drove her, in the sailors on the deck, and in the captain on the bridge. There was fascination for me in the casting-off at Glasgow and in the "tie-up" at Belfast; in the ships we passed at sea, in the lighthouses which flashed their messages through the darkness; in the stars, and in the moon, and even in the wind and waves. I felt that the world was being opened up to me. That it was good to be alive and better still to be a cabin-boy on a gallant Clyde-built steamship.

In the light of the dazzling new experiences now unfolding before me I began to let my fancy roam much further afield than the quayside at Belfast. How splendid it would be, I kept saying to myself, to sail across the Atlantic to America! I often heard the passengers speak about New York, and Philadelphia, and Boston, and Chicago, and the prairies and the cotton-fields. Glorious names and fascinating vistas! Some members of the crew had made trips to America and they also never tired of telling of its vastness, its wealth, the boundless opportunities which the great new world across the Western Ocean was offering with open hands to all and sundry. Fortunes were to be picked up for the asking. Millionaires grew up at the rate of one a day! I listened eagerly to all this and made up my mind sooner or later to try my luck in America.

The opportunity came much sooner than I expected. On arrival at the Broomielaw one morning the shore steward's representative came on board. He was evidently in a bad temper for among other things he complained that one of the cabin lamps had been allowed to smoke and discolour the white enamel of the ceiling. Who was to blame! "Young Lipton!" said the Chief Steward. I was given a week's notice on the spot! But once more the tables were turned by the passage of time. For

I have often been entertained, during the Clyde yachting "fortnights", by the late Lord Inverclyde, Chairman of the Burns Line of steamers on one of which I once worked as a cabin-boy! At dinner on his yacht, or when he came to dine on mine, we have repeatedly laughed over the old story.

CHAPTER IV

Off to America in the steerage—the old Devonia—
*first glimpses of New York—work in the tobacco
plantations of Virginia—a change over to rice—I turn
correspondent for an amorous Spaniard—and nearly
lose my life—a sea trip and salvage—I turn fireman at
fifty cents an hour.*

I WASTED no time in vain regrets. I had saved a
few pounds out of my wages and "tips" and before
I went home that morning, I made inquiries as to
the cost of a steerage passage and the dates of sail-
ings for New York. At one time I had the idea to
set sail without telling my mother and father, as I
apprehended the usual objections from them to a
mere lad going abroad. But I could not bring
myself to this course. It would not be playing the
game. So I went home, told them what had
happened, and urged them with all the pleading I
could to let me go to America, the Land of Promise.
My enthusiasm won the day. The parting was sad,
but I really think that my mother, at least, had such
faith in me that she believed I would soon return
a rich man.

Whenever I find myself on one of the crack
Atlantic liners like the *Leviathan,* or the *Majestic,*
or the *Berengaria,* or the *Aquitania,* my memory
wanders back to the trip I made, over sixty years

ago, in the steerage quarters of the old Anchor liner *Devonia*. She was considered a fine vessel in her day but would have made little more than a tender to the speedy and magnificent floating hotels in which I now make my voyages to the States. The *Devonia* took so long to cross from Glasgow that some of the steerage passengers were sure the captain had lost his way. But at last we hauled in at Castle Garden. I had only thirty shillings in my pocket and many of the other emigrants had considerably less. As the boarding-house keepers were touting for patrons among the passengers by shouting the quality of their accommodation from the quay I hit upon a novel plan. It was a mere notion rather than a plan, but I instantly put it into execution. Running down the gangway well ahead of the early landers I hustled round among the canvassers until I came across rather a decent looking man with a distinct Irish brogue. I drew this chap aside—his name was Mike McCauligan and his address 27½ Washington Street, New York—and whispered to him:

"I have many friends on board and great influence with them. What will you charge me if I bring you a dozen lodgers to-night?"

"Not a cent, me bould lad," said Mike, "I'll board you free for a week!"

Back on board I rushed and from amongst a certain group with whom I had been popular because I wrote their letters home for them (few of

A COPY OF THE ORIGINAL LIPTON ONE-POUND NOTES WHICH, PRINTED
AND DISTRIBUTED IN MILLIONS, PROVED TO BE A SENSATIONALLY
SUCCESSFUL ADVERTISEMENT, EVEN IF THE "NOTES" DID LEAD TO
ALL SORTS OF TROUBLE IN UNEXPECTED QUARTERS

the steerage passengers were able to read or write)
I soon collected round me, to Mike's delight, a
baker's dozen instead of the promised twelve.

The McCauligan boarding-house was anything
but a Biltmore or a Waldorf-Astoria.

I saw many strange sights and took part in
a few exciting scenes. The human flotsam and
jetsam of New York of the 'sixties rolled in and out
of the house. But though I had only reached my
fifteenth birthday soon after landing in America,
I was old enough to realize that any sort of roof
over my head was better than none at all. Often
we slept eight in a room o' nights. The boarders
were drawn from all nationalities under the sun,
and unless when a row sprang up, which was not
infrequent, there was very little talking for the
good and sufficient reason that hardly anybody
understood his neighbour's language. The old
Washington Street that I knew has been demolished
and Mike McCauligan's is no more. Hardbitten old
Mike himself must have gone the way of all flesh—
even of the New York type of which he was a not
unfascinating example.

I was advised to put my name down in an
employment registry office and in due course I got
the offer of a job on a tobacco plantation in
Dinwiddy County, Virginia. The clerk at the
registry office asked me if I thought I would like
it. The very name "Virginia" appealed to me (it
always has, as a matter of fact) and I replied that

I was taking the job just as soon as I could get at it. The same evening I set off for the tobacco fields of the south, full of hope and high spirits. To reach my destination, which was Wilsons' Depot, I travelled by way of City Point on the St. James's River and then on to Petersburg. I had only a few dimes in my pocket but this did not prevent me taking a keen interest in the journey, and I remember as if it were yesterday how tremendously impressed I was by the new and wonderful country in which I now found myself. The planter to whom I was due to start work was one, Sam Clay. I liked him from the start. He passed me over to his manager and I commenced work in the tobacco fields forthwith.

Hard though this new job was, I liked it and thrived on it, for everyone was kind and considerate. I and my fellow-toilers trudged home every night to the little cabin where we lodged, so tired and weary that we were glad, our hunger appeased by a square meal, to sink down and forget our exhaustion in almost instantaneous sleep. Take my word for it, there was no restless tossing on the beds of that Virginian cabin; its occupants slept like logs until it was time to tumble out for another day's "hard darg", as we say in Scotland. But by each mail, I used to write home that I was getting on fine and saving money—which was quite true. For, noticing that I was big and strong, the foreman promoted me to still harder work and as this carried increased wages I was only too willing to tackle it. Months elapsed and every week I added a bit to my store of savings. The more I earned the more I saved.

Then one day an accident befell me which for a time looked like stopping my career in the States, at least as an able-bodied, young man. I was cutting wood one blazing morning when the hatchet slipped and severely injured my right foot. News of the accident was sent to Sam Clay and the kindly planter, instead of sending me to my straw bed in the cabin, had me removed to his own comfortable house. For weeks I suffered great agony, only relieved by the knowledge imparted by the doctor that I was not going to lose my foot. The boss and his splendid wife nursed me back to convalescence and they could not have treated me better had I been their own son. As soon as I was able to hobble about again they insisted on my taking things easy and even drove me to church with them on Sundays. It is a real joy to me to-day to be able to pay a tribute to Sam Clay and his wife, of Dinwiddy County, Virginia. Let me also add that not long ago I had the immense joy of entertaining at Osidge, my home on the outskirts of London, a granddaughter of my first American employer, Sam Clay. His name stands high with me and always has done.

When I was quite fit I went back to the tobacco-fields. But somehow the accident to my foot had

taken all the zest out of me and after a few weeks
I went to my employer and told him that I would
like to try my hand at something else. He was
very nice about it, and quite agreed that the tobacco-
fields did not offer any great chance of advance-
ment for an ambitious youth with his way to make
in the world. Mr. Clay asked me what I had in
mind, and I had to confess that the only settled
notion I had was to get back to New York—that
tremendous city which, all my life, has been like a
lode-star to me as it has been to millions of
others.

I had saved up a good few dollars so that I
faced the next few weeks with confidence. To see
some of the country on my way back to L'il Old
New York—the phrase described New York much
better then than it does now!—was an idea I had
harboured for many weeks and I now took advantage of the opportunity. For instance, I spent a
day or two at Virginia and visited the home of
Jefferson Davis and the Hollowwood Cemetery.
Young as I was I remember with what eagerness
I visited all the historic spots around Virginia; it
seemed to my mind that I was walking on holy
ground indelibly associated with the glorious early
romance of the vast new land, the new people, and
the new spirit amongst which I now found myself
a very humble but admiring unit. At nights I lived
in the cheapest boarding-houses I could discover.
Even then this holiday appeared to me to be wildly

extravagant, but I revelled in every minute of it.

On arriving back at New York I thought it would be easy to pick up a job of some kind or another. As it happened, however, I seemed to have struck the old town during a temporary lull in the employment market. As day after day passed and my small remaining hoard of dollars melted down to a few dimes and nickels I became very depressed. Just when things were at their blackest the agency which had sent me to Sam Clay's place had a few vacancies for strong, able-bodied young fellows on a rice plantation in South Carolina. So I again headed South.

This time, my employers were Willis & Chisholm, then well-known planters at Coosaw Island on the Edisto River, sixty miles from Charleston and forty from Savannah. Yet once more new vistas and strange, wonderful scenes were opened up to me on the journey to the sunny south and my mind was again fortified with a sense of the magnitude and future of the astounding country known as the United States. On the map in my little geography book at school, and also on the larger one which I had bought in order to study the world-trips of the ships coming to Glasgow harbour, the "U.S.A." had appeared to be a very large territory as compared with our own little islands, but it was only after I had started to travel in the new country that I began to realize its immensity. I found myself comparing the passage from Glasgow to Belfast on the Burns liner with the journey from New York to Charleston and, after that, asking myself what sort of distance must lie between the Carolina town and, say, San Francisco! I recollect my imagination reeling at the probable answer.

I started work the very day I arrived at Coosaw Island. Here, I made my home in a cabin, occupied by a Spaniard and his wife. The former was a decent, likeable fellow and his wife was an Irish-woman who took quite a fancy to me. We were the best of friends all round. One day, in a burst of confidence the Spaniard told me of an incident in his life which had happened two or three years before. It appeared that during the Civil War, he had been stationed as a soldier at Fort Sumter and there, faithful husband as he assured me he had always been and would always be, the little god Cupid had played rather a mean trick on him. He had been attracted more than he should have been by a pretty girl and she, in her turn, had fallen in love with this dark-eyed son of Spain.

The disturbing feature of this domestic drama was that the Spaniard and his lady friend still cor-responded. Now, would I be willing to help him so far as his side of the letter-writing was con-cerned? Being too young to understand the dangers of the situation, I agreed, and that night, stealing together into the woods near by our cabin,

I wrote for him the desired letter, and pending the departure of the mail for Charleston I undertook to keep the missive in my pocket. I put it there and forgot all about it.

Next day, on the Spaniard asking me if I had posted his letter, I was amazed to find that it had gone from my pocket. We were both in much apprehension that his wife had purloined it and went home for our evening meal of homminy and rice with quaking hearts. Sure enough, the bombshell fell. Immediately after the wife had cleared away the dishes she turned to her man and upbraided him bitterly for his deception. Quick action followed. The hot-blooded Spaniard, convinced that I had betrayed him, turned on me and before I realized what was happening he had drawn a knife from his belt and slashed me across the face with it. Only my agility and fleetness of foot prevented me from being murdered. Dodging the infuriated man, I rushed to the door and out of the cabin. He pursued me all the way to the overseer's house. Fortunately, Mr. Mathews, the overseer, was on the spot and he not only gave me instant shelter, but held off the enraged Spaniard with a loaded revolver. My wounds were dressed and I remained with Mr. Mathews that night. In the morning the Spaniard came up with profuse apologies. His wife, fully believing that her husband had killed me, told him that she had been suspicious of us going off to the woods together, taking the ink-bottle and pen with us, and that after we had gone to sleep she had searched our pockets and found the letter. The whole dramatic incident had a happy ending. Husband and wife agreed to let bygones be bygones; they implored me to return to their cabin, which I did, and the three of us were the best possible friends for the rest of the time I remained on the rice-fields.

Perhaps Mr. Mathews had formed a favourable opinion of me in connection with the settling-up of this "shindy" with the Spaniard; at all events I was promoted to the plantation office as accountant and book-keeper. This job, coming after months of hard, physical work in the fields, was a wonderful bit of luck. It gave me an opportunity to expand in a new direction, to equip myself just a little better for the battle of life. I had a natural aptitude, I found, for figures and my skill in penmanship was given full scope. I did my level best to keep the plantation books better than they had ever been kept before. All through life I have discovered that the boy or the man who can do things even a shade better than the other fellow is the one to whom the plums will fall sooner or later. This is obvious, I can hear some of my readers say. It is, but nevertheless it is astonishing how many people miss the obvious in life and in business. I held my book-keeper's job down for almost a twelve-month.

But once again I got that "restless feelin'", the

urge for something bigger and better, and I began to cudgel my brains as to how I could get away from Coosaw Island and a business where there was only hard work, little money and no future. The chance came in due course. One day a big sailing schooner put in at one of the island anchorages not far from our rice-farm. I heard she was bound for Charleston and immediately I made up my mind to interview her captain and ask to be allowed to work my passage to the mainland town. I met another boy who also wanted to get away and together we had a chat with the skipper—a genial chap who was not averse to helping us, "but," he said, "you must not let anybody know a word about it. Otherwise I shall get into trouble."

The captain also clearly gave us to understand that we would have to board the ship after nightfall. This seemed to present rather a difficulty but I remembered a little canoe, the property of the Spaniard, in which I had frequently gratified my love for sailing. This would have to be "borrowed" for the occasion. Besides, the son of Spain owed me something, I argued, for that uncalled-for attack with his knife. About nine o'clock in the evening the other boy and myself stole down to the water's edge, embarked in the canoe and soon found ourselves on the deck of the schooner which sailed away a few minutes afterwards. My farewell to the rice plantation on Coosaw Island might have taken place in more conventional circumstances, I felt, and I was sorry not to have said good-bye to Mr. Mathews, the overseer, but the chance to make a get-away was too good to be missed. And, once aboard the tall schooner, the sense of high adventure was again upon me.

On the passage to Charleston we called at a real desert island. Totally uninhabited, it would have proved an ideal spot for the landing of a modern Robinson Crusoe. Spread along the shores of the island were many piles of carefully-cut wood, evidently collected and stacked by some person or persons whose idea was to return and ship the material to the mainland. Our skipper, however, acted upon the principle that "findings were keepings" and his crew, assisted by the two stowaways, were kept busy for hours transferring the wood to the deck of the schooner. It proved valuable "salvage" at Charleston.

When we arrived at the great Carolina port, it was to discover the entire population seething with excitement over a disastrous fire which had broken out the previous day and was still raging and threatening the complete destruction of the town. This was bad luck for Charleston and thousands of its citizens, but it was good luck for me because I immediately got a job with one of the fire-engine squads at fifty cents an hour! I became an enthusiastic fireman at this remunerative pay and would not have minded very much had the conflagration lasted a month. But it was all out in a day or two, and soon my boy friend and myself were tramping the streets and docks looking for work. An occasional odd job or two came our way, but the fire, instead of causing employment, had the reverse effect, and in no time at all we were penniless.

CHAPTER V

I stow away on a tramp steamer—empty pockets and no work—a change in my fortunes—I become assistant in a prosperous grocery-store in New York—the idea fascinates—back to Glasgow to see "the old folks at home"—unusual gifts for my mother—a drive down Crown Street in style.

Moodily walking along the quayside, we came abreast of a steamer called the *Moneka*, taking on the last of her cargo for New York. A sudden longing to be back there again seized me. And the longing inspired an idea. Great bales of cotton were being pushed on board across a flat gangway. Why not help to push one on board—and stay on board? I suggested this to my chum. Instantly he gave the plan his blessing. The ruse worked splendidly. In less time than it takes to tell, we were both on the good ship *Moneka* and making ourselves as scarce as we knew how in the steerage quarters. There we contrived to remain hidden until the ship had not only sailed but had dropped her pilot at Fort Sumter.

The purser's face was a study, some hours later, when we boldly reported ourselves to him and asked to be given some work to do in return for our passage to New York! It was my idea to make a clean breast of our presence aboard—carrying the war into the enemy's camp, so to speak. We were speedily taken before the captain, and here again my candour and straightforward admissions seemed to impress him. In any event, he told me off for work on the deck and the other boy was sent below to help the stokers. I think I had the better share of the "punishment"!

Back once again to New York! The companion with whom I had travelled all the way from Coosaw Island, and for whom I had developed a real liking —as people will do for those introduced to them by adversity—went home to his father and mother, and for the third time I found myself alone in the big city. For New York I have always had an extremely soft side. Many of the happiest days of my life have been spent there. I have countless good friends there. I never tire of New York; it has a fascination peculiarly its own. All the same, I must admit that on this occasion I experienced a very thin time of it. I had not much money in my pocket, and New York, like most other places, does not offer a boisterously warm welcome to the man or boy with a decided scarcity of dollars in his possession. Trade had not yet begun to recover from the effects of the Civil War, and in the cities, particularly, employment was difficult to secure. For several days after stepping off the *Moneka* I tried to find a billet, but without success, so once again I shook the dust of Broadway off my feet and took the long trail.

For the next few months I wandered over different parts of the States, taking a job at this thing or the next, and passing on when the work was finished or I felt that I could better myself. Always, for some unexplained reason, I seemed to gravitate south. Perhaps I liked the warmth! By and by I landed at Carlton, seven miles from New Orleans. Here I was lucky to get a berth with the local tram-car company, and equally fortunate to find good lodgings with the wife of the foreman of the car-yard. This lady, to whom I paid five dollars a week for my board and lodging, was an exceedingly kind and motherly person. She took a great fancy to me, and her face beamed with pleasure when I told her that the pancakes she made were "just like my mother's". This "pancake" story has an interesting little sequel.

Fully forty years afterwards I happened to be at New Orleans—in the autumn of 1912, to be exact—and this time I was staying with my party at the St. Charles Hotel at a cost of, figuratively speaking, five dollars a minute, as against the five dollars a week I paid for my lodgings when first I struck the town! The next morning after my arrival I was looking out of my bedroom window and ruminating on the changed conditions under which I was making my second visit to the magnificent city on the Mississippi, when the bell-hop came

LADY: "NO WONDER LIPTON IS A BACHELOR IF THAT'S HIM!"

up with the announcement that an old lady who knew me as a boy had called to pay her respects to me. I went downstairs wondering who this could be, and was delighted beyond measure to discover that it was none other than my old landlady from Carlton. She had followed my career all through the years, and learning from the papers that I was in New Orleans, had made up her mind to come and see me. You may be sure I gave her a very fine welcome, and at lunch that day she was my most honoured guest. During the meal she leaned over the table and said: "Do you remember saying, Sir Thomas, that my pancakes were every bit as good as those your mother used to make?" Laughingly I replied that I not only remembered saying it, but that I remembered the pancakes even better. This meeting was for me a most refreshing link with the past; and I can truthfully say that in all America there was no one with whom I would rather have renewed my friendship than with this dear old lady.

I feel I could go on indefinitely recalling these youthful experiences in different parts of the States, but I must really pass on to the chain of events which had so much influence in moulding my whole future career. Eventually, I returned to New York where I was fortunate in obtaining a post as an assistant in a prosperous grocery-store. Here, at last, was a business that appealed to me. I liked it from the outset. I could see possibilities in it.

People must eat, I told myself, and the store that tempted people to buy good goods would never be empty of customers. Certainly our store was a busy place; it was run on up-to-date methods. These I studied keenly all the time I was employed there. I thought I could see subtle differences between shopkeeping in America as compared with the methods of the tradespeople in Glasgow. The wares offered, the food sold, might not be any better, but it seemed to me that they were "shown" to fuller advantage, the assistants took a more personal interest in the customers they served; in short, there was an "atmosphere" in a New York shop even in those days which seemed to me to invite trade and hold it.

Promotion came to me rapidly in the store. Probably I would have done very well there had I stuck to it, but about this time a tremendous longing assailed me to see my father and mother again. This feeling became overpowering as the months went on. So I saved all the money I could from my wages, and when I had five hundred dollars I booked my passage for Glasgow. My great longing was to see "the old folks at home", but, looking back now over the years, I think I must have had some undefined resolve to apply my American experiences and wit-sharpening adventures to whatever should befall me on my return to my native land. I did not know it at the time, but, as events proved. I went home to make my fortune, thus reversing the usual order of things, whereby emigrant lads have gone to America from all corners of the earth to improve their lot.

To go back to my mother empty-handed would be an impossible thing. I must take her a gift, or gifts, to prove how successful I had been across the seas! What should these gifts consist of? Their selection cost me many hours of anxious consideration. And if you made ten thousand guesses, I don't think you could name the articles. They were a barrel of flour and an American rocking-chair!

The steamship on which I re-crossed the Atlantic arrived at Glasgow early on a Saturday morning. Of course, I should have hurried ashore the moment the vessel tied up and dashed home to my parents. But instead I hatched and carried out a scheme to make my home-coming a much more spectacular affair. Waiting on board the ship until the hour when I knew most of my old companions would be returning from their work, I then hired a cab. Placing the barrel of flour and the rocking-chair on the top of the vehicle, I told the driver to proceed to the end of Crown Street and then drive slowly through that thoroughfare. My plan could not have worked better. Leaning out of the window of the cab, I saluted all my friends with a shout and a cheery wave of the hand. Thus my return caused quite a sensation among my friends. Needless to say, my parents were overjoyed to have me back.

Far into that night and again on the Sunday we sat round the fire while I told them the stories of my adventures. And when my mother said that her rocking-chair was the most comfortable thing she had ever sat in, I felt that all my hardships and hard work had been well worth while.

CHAPTER VI

I assist in my parents' shop—and spring a startling proposition—a deal in hams—I open my first shop in Stobcross Street, Glasgow—first day's record takings— a link with Glasgow University—starting work at six o'clock in the morning—my first assistant buys a new suit and fails to turn up again.

ON the Monday morning I started work as an assistant in the wee butter-and-ham shop. I was now quite a young man, tall and strong, and the old shop seemed very small indeed. But on my return, trade began to improve and soon my mother had quite a tidy bank balance on the right side. I had a good few pounds of my own, and this knowledge caused me to begin dreaming the dreams which I was so soon to translate into realities.

For a long time I hesitated about broaching the subject of "extension" to my father and mother, but, as the business increased and showed a gradually rising profit, I began to feel that no time should be lost in striking out in a bold attempt to improve the family position and prospects. Moreover, I was taking a very keen personal interest in the business. I instituted lots of little ideas for cementing the relationships between customers and ourselves, did most of the buying and all the window-dressing in addition to the serving. When, one memorable day,

I discovered that there was exactly one hundred and one pounds to our credit in the bank, I decided to take the bull by the horns and insist on this large sum of money being used to the fullest advantage.

That same evening I sprang my bombshell on father and mother. "Look here," I said, "what is the use of money lying in the bank? It is doing no good there. Why not let me open a shop and start trading on my own account? Money makes money. But it only makes money rapidly if it is used properly. We are doing as well in the Crown Street shop as we can ever hope to do. If I open another shop, I can double the profits!"

My parents were staggered at the idea. I do believe for a moment or two they thought that I had gone clean "out of my wits". What?—risk all the hard-won savings of years in a wild-cat scheme of starting another shop with all the worry and anxiety which another business would entail! Not on any consideration! The project over which I ha⅃ so fondly built my castles in the air had perforce to be abandoned for the time being. I resolved, however, to raise it again at the first likely opportunity. This came sooner than I had anticipated.

A steamer from Philadelphia arrived at Glasgow after an exceedingly stormy passage. Owing to the delay on the voyage, portions of the cargo were advertised to be sold off in lots, on the quayside, for what they would bring. Fate determined that

I should read this advertisement, and Fate, as I see it, equally determined that hams and bacon should be the first portions of the cargo to meet my eyes on wandering down to the old Broomielaw on the day of the auction sale.

I had a few pounds in my pocket drawn from the bank in case of eventualities, and with this money I became proprietor of a fairly large consignment of hams and bacon, all of which afterwards I sold to small shopkeepers in Glasgow side-streets and made a profit of eighteen pounds. This was my first "fling" in the world of business. Its complete success greatly encouraged me. Repeatedly I kept telling myself that if I could make eighteen pounds by selling a few hams, I could make hundreds of pounds by selling a thousand of them. The operation was the same; the quantities didn't matter. All that *did* matter was the possession of vision, determination, quickness to see an opening and to seize a chance. Success and fortune seldom came stalking up one's home street, uninvited, I told myself. No, you had to go out and meet them more than half-way.

Arguments on these lines I sedulously introduced in my talks with both father and mother, hoping that in time they might relent in their ultra-cautious business outlook. Always my father shook his head.

"We are only humble folks, Tom," he would say, "and we should be thankful that we have done so well. If we followed your plan, people would say that we were riding for a fall, that the peas were shooting above the sticks. Come back to earth, my boy, and stop building castles in the air."

On the other hand, my mother was more inclined to listen to me as time went on. When we were together, I outlined to her my big idea for starting not only one shop but shops all over Glasgow.

"Who knows, mother," I remember saying to her once, "but that there may be a Lipton shop in every city in Scotland! But I must begin soon before any other person gets the same idea. If we can make three pounds profit a week in one shop, I can make six pounds in two and thirty pounds in ten. The main thing to-day is to get the second shop started." And I proceeded to tell her about an empty shop in Stobcross Street on which I had had my eye for a few weeks. At this stage I don't think I would have had any difficulty in persuading my mother to let me embark on my own. My father was more dubious.

In order to let him have a concrete example of what I meant by up-to-date business methods, I did a daring thing. It cost me a good few of the sovereigns I had saved up, but before I committed myself to the scheme I was convinced that it was a sound business "proposition". One morning there drove up to the corner of the wee shop in Crown Street a smart, newly-painted grocer's van with the word "LIPTON" painted along each side, and

LIPTON'S
LEADING
ARTICLE

THE FIRST PICTORIAL ADVERTISEMENT UTILIZED BY LIPTON

One of the earliest cartoons displayed in Lipton's shop

"WHAT'S THE MATTER WITH THE PIG. PAT?"
"SURE, SIRR, HE'S AN ORPHAN SO, OUT OF PITY, I'M TAKING HIM
TO LIPTON'S!"

between the shafts was a smart little horse in a shining set of brand-new harness.

My father was standing at the door when the equipage drew up. I kept in the background and watched him with anxious eyes and a beating heart.

"What on earth does this mean?" I heard him ask the man in charge as the latter jumped down from the van and saluted him.

"It's your new horse and van ordered by your son, sir!" replied the man. "And I must say that it's a fine smart turn-out and does your son credit."

"Well, I don't want anything to do with it," promptly said my father, "and you can take it back to where it came from!"

Without another word he turned into the shop. Later in the day it was my awkward task to go back on my bargain with Messrs. Leckie & Co., the saddlers in Stockwell Street, from whom I had ordered the outfit. "But never fear," I told them, "I shall soon want the horse and van myself, as I am opening up on my own account in Stobcross Street very shortly."

This incident of the horse and van broke down my father's last scruples about letting me have my business head. My mother openly turned in my favour, pointing out to her husband that it was better to have a son who was pushful, self-reliant, and ambitious than one who would simply be content to accept things as they were. Besides, she argued, the boy had looked after himself for three years in America and had been of great assistance in building up the Crown Street business. For her part, she thoroughly believed in Tom and his ability to make good. And that was that!

So it came about that on my twenty-first birthday I started business on my own account in a small shop in Stobcross Street, Glasgow. Here it was that I commenced my career as a merchant. The capital I put into the venture was exactly one hundred pounds. But of this sum I expended less than half on furnishings and stock-in-trade, keeping the balance for contingencies and extensions.

I worked tremendously hard to have the shop spick and span against the opening day. The premises were painted and redecorated inside and out, and I introduced many new ideas in the way of fittings and general equipment. But it was to the stock I paid most attention. Most of it came direct from Ireland, and it was purchased at such keen rates that on my opening day I was announcing prices which quickly caused a sensation amongst my competitors all over the district. Indeed, when it became known that I was offering good ham at fivepence and sixpence per pound, with an "extra special" brand at sevenpence—my opponents hurried along to Stobcross Street to find out who was undercutting them so drastically. Before I had been open many hours there were little crowds round my window, and they didn't all stay outside, either! My first day's drawings were two pounds, six shillings—considerably more than we had ever drawn in a single day at the wee shop in Crown Street.

Stobcross Street was then, as it still is, right in the heart of a densely-populated district of central Glasgow. The street is lined on each side by tall tenements occupied by respectable working people. In the days of which I am writing there were many small shops in the street, but I saw to it that my premises were the brightest and most attractive in the thoroughfare. I kept the place scrupulously clean, I wore white overalls and apron, and when there were no customers to serve I went outside and polished the window. This gave me an opportunity to give a cheery "good day" or "good evening" to any of the housewives passing up and down the street, and occasionally to draw their attention to some tit-bit or another in the window which I could "strongly recommend". As often as not they were prevailed upon to enter the shop and become purchasers. When night came on I did not spare the gas, and Lipton's shop flashed like a beacon, inviting the attention of all and sundry in the long street.

I worked late and early. I was manager, shop-man, buyer, cashier, and message-boy all in one. If I had provisions to collect off the Irish boats, I went down to the quay myself with a hand-cart early in the mornings; if my customers wanted anything sent to their homes, I shut up the shop temporarily and delivered them in person.

On that proudest day in my life, when I was presented with the freedom of my native city of Glasgow in 1923, I drove, together with an old friend who had known me in my early days, past the fine spacious buildings of Glasgow University, and at once these days of my youth came vividly back to me.

"How well I remember attending this University daily when a lad!" I said with a sigh. Hearing this little speech, my old friend looked pained. University education, indeed! Hitherto he had known me as "a man with no frills". Could it be that I was now "putting on side"? Seeing his perplexity, I then explained.

"Surely you, of all people, have not forgotten that I passed through Glasgow University," I said. "Regularly as clockwork every morning for three years I passed through it on my way to deliver groceries at the door of the kitchens, which then used to be at the top of the building!" Then we both laughed heartily!

I do not need to say that my whole heart was in my first little shop. For me at that time, I can assure you, there was no throwing down tools at 6.0 p.m. sharp—no watching the clock for the hour to leave off. I didn't work like that in my youth. I got it into my head that a man could attain almost anything he liked, if only he had the mind. So I stuck to my work all day long and far into the night. Often I was on duty from six in the morning until midnight. Frequently, indeed, I slept in the little back shop so that I could be up bright and early next morning to take advantage of some bargain in butter, or eggs, or bacon which I knew would be on offer. But the work was a thrill and a joy to me. I lived for my little business.

It stands to the credit of my parents that from the first day of my going to Stobcross Street they never interfered with me in any way, not even with suggestions. "You're doin' fine, Tom," was all my mother would say, "but dinna kill yersel' workin' ower hard!"

In six weeks' time the business had made such progress that I had to hire a boy to assist me. He ran the messages and did the odd jobs about the premises. But he was very shabbily dressed. As a matter of fact, his suit was so threadbare and patched that he did not fit in with my scheme of things at all. A ragged boy in my beautiful shop was so completely out of place that one day I put my hand in the till and took out a bright golden sovereign.

"There, Jim," I said, "go and buy yourself a decent suit and put it on during your dinner-hour!"

The boy literally jumped for glee. Sure enough, he returned at two o'clock wearing his new clothes, and I must say he was a credit to the establishment. Next morning, however, Jim failed to show face.

At the end of three days I went and interviewed his mother. "Is your son not well?" I asked her when she answered my knock on the door. "Oh, yes, sir," was the reply, "but he looked so respectable in the new suit you were kind enough to give him that he has now got a better job!"

My second assistant also made a short stay in my employment. Four days after joining my service I sent him out to buy five shillings' worth of half-penny stamps to put on some circulars I had printed—my first attempt at advertising—and when he returned I asked him for the five shillings change out of the half-sovereign I had given him.

"There's no ony change, Mr. Lipton," he coolly remarked, "the price of stamps has riz!"

By and by, however, I found more reliable assistants, some of whom were destined to be associated with me for many years and to rise to important positions in my organization.

The story of how I came to engage the first of these assistants may be worth telling. Walking over Stockwell Bridge one day, my head full of castles in the air as usual, I noticed a strong, vigorous youth of about eighteen pushing a barrow, full to overflowing of ironmongery tools and other merchandise, up the incline of the bridge. The lad was making heavy weather of his task, for there must have been at least half a ton of goods on the barrow, yet he was putting his shoulder to the wheel with right good will. I liked the look of the boy and promptly went to his assistance. Together we trundled the barrow over the bridge.

Naturally, we fell a-talking. He told me that he was employed by a firm in Crown Street, that the work was hard but that he enjoyed it. And he kept smiling all the time. An idea suddenly struck me.

"What wages do you get?" I asked him.

"Seven shillings a week," was his reply. I gave him another look up and down.

"Come and work for me and I'll give you fourteen shillings a week," I said.

"Right you are!" he agreed.

That young man became, in after years, one of my principal directors!

Soon the help of good assistants left me free to indulge in my dreams of expansion. I did not abate one jot or tittle of my enthusiasm or concentration on the essential details of business, but I began to cast my mind out and beyond the confines of Stobcross Street. In other words, I was beginning to realize that the first aim in business is to secure more business, and also that the more business you can do the less profit you can work on. Simplified down to the elemental truths, I realized that it was far better to make a small profit on a turnover of say a thousand pounds, than a slightly larger profit on a turnover of half that amount.

My first important "deal" on these lines came to a head when I secured the contract to supply provisions for the staff of one of the largest drapery firms in Glasgow. When my assistant heard that I was intent on tendering for such a contract, he was astounded at my presumption.

"They'll never give it to a wee shop like ours, Mr. Lipton," he said. "You'll just get a disappointment. Don't try to run before you can walk."

"Just see how fast I am going to run on this contract," was all I said. "The other firms won't see my feet for dust!"

So I sat down and drew up quotations for first-class goods at prices which left me only the barest margin of profit. I was determined not to be undercut by any other shop. And along with my tender I sent daintily packed samples of the quality of ham, butter, eggs, etc., I was prepared to supply. Confronted by such enterprise the directors of the drapery establishment at once gave me the contract. Naturally, I did not hide my light under a bushel, and I made as much capital as possible out of the fact that "Lipton's" were supplying the famous firm of So-and-so with their household provisions. Other similar contracts were secured in due time. All the goods came through the little shop in Stobcross Street, and you may imagine how hard I and my one assistant had to work to keep step with the growth of the business.

CHAPTER VII

I realize the power of advertisement—posters and a swinging, painted ham to a live, be-ribboned pig parading the streets—the "Lipton Orphans"—a foundation to fortune—my association with Willie Lockhart, cartoonist—statuary in butter—I take a trip to Ireland for supplies and pawn my watch—decide to take up French—a bout with the German master from which I emerge victorious, but with very little French.

BUT although hard work was, undoubtedly, a big factor in the building up of my business, I realize that it would have counted for little if, even at this very early stage of my career, I had not been quick to grasp how great can be the Power of Advertisement. The trouble in the 'seventies was that few people could be induced to take advertising seriously. It has frequently been said that I was one of the earliest pioneers in the movement which brought about the stupendous change whereby advertising now ranks as one of the most highly-specialized and essential branches of British and American business. And however that may be, it is certainly true that I was one of the first Britishers to see the immense possibilities and advantages to be reaped from novel and judicious advertising.

Even in these early days I found myself toying with the idea of advertising my shop and its wares.

I have told you that of the original hundred pounds capital, I only used about half in starting the shop, the rest remaining on deposit receipt at the bank until such time as I could hit upon some suitable method of employing it. Well, after much serious thought I determined to use a portion of the money in advertising. During my travels in America I had observed that the firms that were making good were all regular advertisers. One couplet I remembered having seen in New York was to the effect that:

> "The man who on his trade relies
> Must either bust or advertise."

And these two simple but effective lines kept constantly recurring to my mind.

My first essay in the art of advertising was a very simple handbill urging all housewives who wanted superb value at the lowest possible prices to patronize Lipton's Market in Stobcross Street. Later I posted a circular containing my prices—and asking for a comparison with those of other traders —to a few hundred specially selected addresses in my vicinity. Then I tried a small "ad" in a Glasgow evening newspaper, drawing attention to a line of extra fine bacon to be had at my shop at a price which "defied competition". This advertisement cost me seven shillings and sixpence—the forerunner of many hundreds of thousands of pounds

SIR THOMAS LIPTON AT THE AGE OF 27, ALREADY ON THE WAY
TO FAME AND FORTUNE

spent by the Lipton firm in the newspaper press of the old and new worlds.

But how to discover something really novel in the shape of an advertisement without expending much money? This was my next problem. Hand-bills, smartly-worded window cards, newspaper "inches" or larger spaces were all very well so far as they went, but I was not satisfied that these efforts were sufficient. If I could invent something that would make people talk, or, better still, make them laugh, I would, it seemed to my mind, be much nearer solving the problem of effective advertising. In the opening weeks of my trading I had noticed that a smile and a joke were generally well received by my customers, and I also noted this human characteristic—that people in a good humour will always spend more freely than those with a frown on their face. Therefore, I kept telling myself, the best ideas behind successful advertising must be those with a smile in them. But it was difficult to hit upon just the right notion to begin with; once started, I knew very well that other suggestions would follow automatically.

Suddenly one morning the bright idea struck me that it might be a good thing to have a large wooden ham, painted as realistically as possible, hung from a pole outside the shop door. Nobody passing up or down the street could miss the sign and insignia of the shop's principal contents. I had the idea carried out forthwith. The swinging ham attracted quite a lot of attention immediately. Indeed, it was far more successful than I had imagined, for it was put up on a very hot day, the sun promptly melted the paint on the ham, and, lo and behold! the latter became an almost perfect example of a large, luscious ham straight from the boiling! It caused endless amusement among the passers-by and soon people came from all over the district to see "Lipton's greasy ham"!

From a single ham to an entire pig was, obviously, an easy step. In fact, two pigs— the largest, fattest, finest porkers I could buy at the Glasgow live-stock market! These I had removed to a private yard and scrubbed and polished until they looked the most respectable pair of hogs ever seen out of Smithfield Show. I put pink and blue ribbons round their necks and tassels on their tails to match, and had them driven through the streets with a large banner suspended over them and bearing the words "Lipton's Orphans". Long before they had arrived opposite the shop in Stobcross Street the pigs had collected a vast crowd. The scheme had been a triumphant success. Everybody asked every other body what the joke was, who the pigs belonged to, and the entire crowd was kept in constant merriment by the antics of the pigs all along the "line of march".

This new method of driving the traditional pigs "to market" was too good to drop. I employed the

same pigs over and over again, but always took
care to see that they followed a different route to
Stobcross Street. A variation of the "stunt" was to
have a typical Irishman, knee-breeches, cutaway
coat, billycock hat, shillelagh an' all an' all, "steer-
ing" an enormous porker through the most crowded
thoroughfares of the city. On the pig's sides were
painted the words: "I'm going to Lipton's. The
best shop in town for Irish Bacon!"

As often as not the Lipton pigs, being the largest
and fattest I could find, took it into their heads to
lie down in the middle of the street and refuse to
budge an inch. At Glasgow Cross on one occasion
a "procession" of "Lipton's Orphans" all decided to
have a siesta together on the tram-lines, and
traffic was entirely suspended for quite a long
time.

There are many people still alive in Glasgow
who will tell you that these orphan-pigs laid the
foundation of my fortunes. In any case I cannot
deny that my idea of advertising by means of live
pigs created a first-class sensation all over the city.
The novelty of the whole thing appealed to people
and made them laugh. My name was on everybody's lips. And that was all I wanted. Customers
came to the shop in ever-increasing numbers, and
in less than six months after I had taken down the
shutters for the first time I had to extend my
premises.

My next novelty in advertising was to secure the

whole-time services of Willie Lockhart, one of the finest cartoonists in Scotland. Willie was a good-natured fellow, but a Bohemian with an artistic temperament who knew nothing of business. The fact that he, of all people, should now join my staff looked like sheer madness to old trade-rivals, and they made it the target for many a joke. "What in the wide world had cartoons to do with selling eggs and bacon?" they asked. They had not to wait long to see.

The first cartoon Lockhart drew for me reduced to paper the same idea of "Lipton's Orphans" as had been used a few days before in the street-processions. It took the form of a large humorous poster which, prominently displayed in the window, drew crowds to the shop. The scene depicted in the cartoon was that of a solitary pig, its eyes streaming with tears, perched on the back of an Irish drover, while near by stood an old lady, full of concern for the animal's grief. And underneath was this letter-press:

OLD LADY: "Why, my good man, what ails your pig?"

THE IRISHMAN: "Sure ma'am, he's an orphan; the rest of the family have gone to Lipton's."

This simple cartoon drew thousands of people to my window, and regularly, thereafter, a fresh cartoon was pasted up every Monday morning. People came from all over the town to look at them, and they always went away with a smile on their faces. One very successful cartoon, I remember, was inspired by the fall of one of the Gladstone Ministries. One half of the picture was devoted to the defeated Cabinet in terribly woe-begone plight, while the other half showed the same statesmen, headed by the illustrious William Ewart Gladstone himself, emerging joyfully from my shop and each brandishing a sturdy ham by its shank. The smile on Mr. Gladstone's face as he gazed aloft at his particular ham made all Glasgow laugh uproariously. I never saw such a comic laugh on any human face; I chuckled myself every time I looked at the cartoon.

The idea behind the cartoon was, of course, that so long as Lipton's Market was to the fore, there was no excuse for prolonged despondency anywhere— not even in a defeated British Cabinet!

Lockhart's drawings were so successful that I put him on to do pictorial price-cards for the goods in the windows. Some of these were most amusing, particularly one entitled: "Great Fall in Eggs." This showed a fat policeman who, foiled in an effort to climb a wall over which a burglar was escaping, had fallen slap into a crate of eggs. It was rumoured that Willie Lockhart had taken for his model a certain Glasgow policeman against whom he had a grudge. Be this as it may, I know that every policeman in the city came to have a look at the picture, and many of them became customers at my shop.

Nor was it solely in cartoons and pictures that Lockhart's gifts found their full artistic scope, for under my guidance and encouragement he blossomed forth into a sculptor on highly original lines. The Lipton "statuary in butter" was soon known far and wide. Lockhart could convert a firkin of butter into a dozen different and pleasing designs; perhaps his greatest triumph in this line being a tableau representing a stout policeman making love to a pretty dairymaid. Lockhart's policemen and all his other male characters— whether drawn by pencil or brush, or built up of butter, cheese—sausages, even—were, without exception, happy-featured, heavy-paunched, and jovial to the last degree. Neither he nor I had any use whatever for skinny, miserable types; these were entirely foreign to our ideas and to the wares sold by Thomas Lipton!

To secure adequate and constant supplies to meet the increasing demands of a rapidly extending body of customers was a problem which I early had to face. At the outset of the business I had, of course, to depend to a great extent on wholesalers, or middlemen, for the goods sold over my counter. But it did not take me long to realize that there was a far more satisfactory way than this. Why not be my own middleman and buy direct from the producers? The advent of more assistants now left me free to attempt direct relationships with the Irish peasants and farmers from whose farms so much of the Glasgow-sold produce originally came. Thus it was that I started making regular trips to the north and west of Ireland. I personally attended the markets in the different towns and villages and paid spot cash for all the stock I wanted. I was sure in this way of getting the best material at the lowest cash price.

A rather curious experience once befell me at a place called Lisnaske, not far from Enniskillen. It was famous for its fine butter, and it so happened that I wanted quite a lot of butter at the time. As a matter of fact, I got much more butter than I wanted! Here is the story. On the journey from Glasgow to Belfast I fell in with an English commercial traveller who was also bound for Lisnaske. We became very friendly. He told me all about himself, and I told him about my business in Glasgow and how I was now doing my own buying in the Irish markets.

"Well, Lipton," said my companion, "I'll put you wise to a wrinkle for taking a rise out of all your rival butter-buyers at Lisnaske market to-morrow morning. I know Lisnaske well and you can collar the market if you do as I tell you!"

I listened to his plan with intense interest. It seemed quite good to me. Next morning I was up betimes and proceeded to put my friend's scheme into operation. First of all I hired a stall in the village square and also a set of scales and some weights from one Noble, the manager of the market. Afterwards I cast round for a smart, alert young man and, having found one, I offered him five shillings if he would go outside the town, meet the farmers on their way in and make deals with them for their butter and eggs before they entered the market. The price I was offering was written down on different tickets, so much for butter and so much for eggs, and these tickets were to be given to the farmers with the information that cash down would be paid by Thomas Lipton, of Glasgow, for all the supplies they cared to take him.

In less than half an hour the farmers began to roll up to my stall, passing, much to their mortification, all the other would-be buyers. I was kept hard at work weighing the butter and counting the eggs and paying out the agreed upon prices. After about two hours' steady business, I was horrified to find that my supply of cash had run out. My competitors were not slow to discover my predicament and they started to jeer at the young merchant from Glasgow who had pulled such a "sharp one" on them. The truth was, however, that I was only thirty shillings short if I was to implement my bargain with the last two or three farmers. I refused to be beaten. I had promised cash down and cash down I would pay. So I stepped across the village square to a pawnbroker's shop and

SIR THOMAS LIPTON AT HIS LONDON OFFICE IN 1897. NOT THEN
FIFTY YEARS OF AGE, HE WAS ALREADY A MULTI-MILLIONAIRE
EMPLOYING MANY THOUSANDS OF PEOPLE

"popped" my silver watch for the vital and necessary thirty shillings!

I had to telegraph home for funds and remain at Lisnaske until the money arrived for me to settle my hotel bill and redeem my watch and chain from the pawnbroker. This was my first and last experience of the inside of a pawn-shop.

As may well be imagined I had very little leisure time on my hands. It was a case of work, work, work from sunrise—and frequently before it—until late at night. But what glorious fun it was! I never felt that I wanted more amusement or excitement than my business afforded me. After the first few months I stopped sleeping in the back-shop and went home to the old rooftree in Crown Street. No matter how late I arrived home, my father and mother were anxious to know what had happened "down at Stobcross Street", what new scheme or idea I had hatched, and generally how things had prospered or gone awry. After supper I would get out an old fiddle and "scrape awa'" for the better part of an hour; if I didn't practise on the violin I would give myself a French lesson, for, at this time in my career, I was most anxious to learn another language or two.

Indeed, I was so full of this zest for self-improvement that I would willingly have spent several hours a day to that end had I been able to spare the time which, of course, I was not. All the same, this did not prevent me once making an arrangement with a certain German gentleman, one, Herr Schultz, to come to the back-shop at Stobcross Street and give me a series of lessons in the Teutonic tongue. I paid him in advance for the lessons. This was a mistake. The wily German did not turn up on the evening we had arranged for the first lesson. Evening after evening went by and still there was no sign of him. My patience becoming exhausted, and my wrath rising in proportion, I went one night in search of this swindling professor. I tracked him down to rooms in the neighbourhood of St. Vincent Street. He was a very astounded man when he personally answered my ring at the door-bell.

"I have been waiting for you to teach me German," I announced without further parleying, "and now I'm going to teach you!" *My* lesson didn't occupy more than five minutes, but it was a good one.

The incident did not end here, however. Next morning my mother happened to be in the shop when Sergeant Swanson, of the Western Police Division, came in and alarmed her dreadfully by telling her that a German professor of languages had lodged a complaint against me for grievous bodily assault. The sergeant, who was a great friend of mine, urged my mother to prevail upon me to make myself scarce for a few days until the affair blew over. This she did with all the pleading at her command. The mere idea of her Tom being "in trouble with the police" badly upset the poor soul. For my part, I was very unwilling to "flee from justice" because I knew I had done no wrong in chastising a swindler; but in the end I decided to clear out temporarily, and I took the train the same day for Dundee.

CHAPTER VIII

*I have to go "in hiding" until the uproar dies down
—and open my first branch shop—others follow—the
difficulties of finding reliable assistants—I aim to open
a new shop every week—dreams for the future.*

WHILE enjoying an enforced holiday in the fine
old Tayside city, I did not waste time, for, while
there, I saw a vacant shop in the Murraygate which
I thought would make a magnificent Lipton Market.
I got the keys from the "factor", examined the
premises and practically completed arrangements to
take them over on a long lease. As a matter of
fact, the final leasing of the shop did not take place
for a considerable time afterwards; but this shop,
as it happened, was my first branch establishment
outside of Glasgow and an exceedingly profitable
venture it proved to be.

When I had been in Dundee four days, I got
a telegram from my mother telling me that I might
safely return home as the police had discovered
Schultz to be a rogue of the first water. He had
swindled many more people than Tom Lipton and
had himself bolted from the city. Far from being
censured for taking the law into my own hands and
administering a sound "leathering" to the rascally
Schultz, I was highly commended for my action;

a well-known Glasgow magistrate even went the length of saying that I had performed a useful public service!

This story is only worth telling at length because the circumstances surrounding it had a very important bearing on my whole future career as a merchant. Had I not gone to Dundee, and had I not taken a determined fancy for that shop in the Murraygate, it is no certainty that I would ever have extended my activities outside the radius of Glasgow. Up till this stage I had more than once pondered over starting another shop as soon as I had saved enough money for the purpose, but it was not until I had visited Dundee that the vision of a nation-wide enterprise—Lipton Stores in every large town in the Kingdom—gradually began to take possession of me.

The old argument I had advanced to my father and mother about two shops, or six shops, or ten shops all being run to show a profit came back to me with doubled force. It was only a question of brains and organization, I told myself; of making profits and conserving them to make other profits in precisely the same way and by the same methods.

Three years after opening the Stobcross Street shop I had sufficient funds in the bank to open another, and much larger, establishment in Glasgow High Street, a mile or thereby to the east of my original premises. In many respects it was a replica of the first, being clean, bright and attractive, with the goods presented in a manner that compelled the attention of the passer-by. This shop was an instantaneous and tremendous success from the outset. A few months later I took over a magnificent shop in Jamaica Street, one of the best shopping thoroughfares in the city, and here again it was a case of scoring an immediate and sensational triumph.

Nothing like "the Lipton Markets", as I had called these establishments, had been seen in Glasgow and it is certain that nothing like the Lipton propaganda or publicity had ever been thought of by any other trader or firm of traders. Press and public combined to applaud my enterprise and originality; the name of Lipton was a household word in a city where, three years before, it had been totally unheard of.

The impetus given to my ambition by the success of these two new shops proved irresistible. But I refused to be carried away into deep waters by a tidal wave of prosperity which might—some people were only too willing to suggest—recede as suddenly as it had sprung up. I had laid my plans so well beforehand that when these sudden developments came along, they did not find me breathless and flustered. From the very first day of trading at Stobcross Street my chief business motto was "cash down; no credit!"—and this, mind you, applied not only to the customer but to myself, for every shop of the many hundreds I was destined to open started without a penny of debt.

Many years ago it was publicly said of me that "Lipton never gambled a penny or backed a bill in his life". The first half of the statement is correct. But there was one occasion in my early career when I did put my name to a bill for a comparatively trifling amount. I forget what the occasion was; if I state that probably I had been buying goods in fairly large quantities and had not sufficient money at the moment to foot the bill I do not think I will be far wrong. At any rate, the thought of this bill became a mill-stone round my neck from the moment I had put my signature to it. I went off my sleep. I couldn't eat. I couldn't work. To my fevered brain those awful words: "One month after date" seemed a phrase of Doom—the Writing on the Wall. Three days after arranging the bill I redeemed it and so restored my peace of mind. I remember to this day the feeling of intense relief with which I tore up the dread document!

There was only one big problem which I feared I would have to face in connection with the opening of these new shops. It was the question of staff, of finding reliable assistants. The general supervision of the branches, the buying, the policy of the business—all these presented no difficulties so long as I could get the right stamp of men and boys. But I need have had no fear on this score, for all my life I have found that there are always plenty of good men everywhere if you only know how to select them and enthuse them with your own ideas. I may have been particularly lucky in my selection of colleagues and assistants in these days, for it is certain that no employer in Glasgow could have had a more loyal band of helpers than I gathered round me in my first three shops! In point of fact I was so satisfied on this score that I went right ahead extending the scope of my operations and in less than five years I was the sole proprietor of twenty establishments in Glasgow and the West of Scotland, all doing a big business and each showing a handsome profit. I celebrated my twenty-sixth birthday by working fourteen hours on the opening day of a new shop in Greenock.

I have already told you how my "compulsory" visit to Dundee some years previously led to opening a branch in that city and it was the phenomenal success of this step which definitely sealed my determination to take the entire United Kingdom as the field of my business operations and make it pay toll to the one-man firm of Thomas Lipton. By this time I had, of course, possessed myself of a central depot—a large, well-equipped building in Lancefield Street, Glasgow, formerly a mill, and here I saw grow up—mushroom-like, I must admit, but based on the most solid foundations—a provision factory compared with which the whole of Scotland had nothing to show.

The organization of this great headquarters

depot kept me engrossed for many months. I was there from early morning until late at night most days of the week. And if I ever did desert my post it was to make a hurried trip to Ireland to buy goods in constantly increasing quantities or to be present at the opening of still another branch in some distant part of the country. This was a rule I set myself in the early days and did not break for many years—the rule that Thomas Lipton in person should be behind the counter on the opening day of every new store. More than that, I made it a practice to serve the first customer myself. By this time my reputation was pretty firmly established, thanks to the Press publicity, which my "modern" methods of shopkeeping had won for me, and thanks also to the unique "advance booms" I organized in each new town marked down for attack; the result was that there was generally a rush of custom the moment the doors were opened. With white jacket and apron, I watched the entrance of the first housewife.

In New York a few months ago I met a very well-known American-Scot, and in the course of conversation he told me that he remembered, as if it were yesterday, the occasion of the opening of my Aberdeen branch in Union Street more than forty-five years ago. His father and mother, according to his story, took him and his young brothers and sisters to see the "wonderfu' new shop, bleezin' wi' lichts, and every man ahint the coonter dressed in white frae heid tae heel!" The old folks had at first no intention of buying anything, being members of the Northern Co-operative Association and keen on the quarterly dividends, but they couldn't resist some of my bargains and the whole family trooped into the new store and, as it so happened, were served by myself. Not only so, but I gave each of the children a new penny—an unheard-of thing for an Aberdeen shopkeeper to do!—and this memorable evening, my friend assured me, had never been forgotten by the family!

Looking back on these days now I often marvel how I found the time for all the things I did. Branches were being opened with clockwork regularity. Property-owners all over the Kingdom wrote to me whenever they had a shop to let. If the town was of any size at all I paid it a visit; it did not take me long to decide one way or the other, and as often as not I arrived by one train and left for home by the first available one thereafter, having in the meantime fixed up all necessary details for opening still another "Lipton Market" or —as occasionally happened—turned the proposition down altogether. While thus engaged extending my activities in every direction I was once asked by a prominent member of Parliament what my political convictions were.

"My politics," I replied, "are to open a new shop every week!" And just at this stage I must have been approaching that very healthy average.

In the admittedly very great business success I found myself achieving before I had reached my thirtieth birthday, I feel I cannot too strongly emphasize once more how much I owed to my firm and persistent faith in the power of advertising. Mr. Gladstone was the great personality in British politics these days. For myself I took not the slightest interest in anything apart from my business but a remark of the Grand Old Man's in a speech at Glasgow appealed to me very much indeed. He said: "Advertising is to business what steam is to industry—the sole propelling power. Nothing except the mint can make money without advertising!" The more I thought of these words the more impressed I was with them. They marched so closely with my own ideas. I have told you some of the earlier ideas which had proved potently effective in drawing the attention of the public to my shops and wares. These, however, were but the preliminaries, merely the heralds, to bigger schemes which I had long had simmering in my brain.

CHAPTER IX

The Lipton pound notes cause a deal of confusion—the Lipton mirrors—the comedy of the fat women and the thin men—the giant "Jumbo" cheese and its triumphant entry into Glasgow—the biggest advertising "stunt" of all—Christmas gold.

ONE of the most spectacular of these was the issue of tens of thousands of "Lipton One Pound Notes". The notes were, outwardly, an almost exact reproduction in size and "feel" of the one pound "bits of paper" issued by a leading Scottish bank. They were so well engraved and printed that at first glance an unsuspecting person might have been excused for regarding them as sound currency. One had only to read the letterpress, of course, to discover that each note was an advertisement in which I, Thomas Lipton, "promise to pay on demand to the bearer at any establishment for fifteen shillings, ham, butter and eggs as offered elsewhere for One Pound sterling!" The broadcast issue of the Lipton Notes caused a sensation and led to many unexpected and comical happenings. Many of the notes found their way into circulation as genuine representations of "real money". Rival shopkeepers found them in their "tills" at night and even the cashiers at one or two Glasgow banks were deceived. I myself was hoist with my own petard for no fewer than five of my own spurious notes were discovered among the takings at my High Street shop one Saturday night!

Travelling in the train one Monday morning from Cambuslang to Glasgow I was given a first-hand example of one use, at least, to which the Lipton notes were being put by highly "philanthropic" Scots. In my compartment were three men to whom I was unknown. They started to speak about the previous night's service in church and extolled the eloquent appeal of the preacher on behalf of the Fund for Clothing the Savages of Rotamagunda—or some such deserving purpose.

"Aye," unctuously remarked the most solemn-faced member of the trio—the Ruling Elder, as I afterwards found out—"It was indeed a searching and a powerful sermon which the meenister delivered. But it deserved a greater response financially than, I am sorry to say, it received!"

"That's funny, Elder," said one of the other men, "for I just said to Jeems here as ye went roond wi' the plate that I never seen sae mony pound in oor collection since the kirk was built!"

"Imphm! That's so," said the Ruling Elder with a sigh. "There were seeven pound notes in the plate, richt enough, but six o' them were Lipton's!"

All sorts of extraordinary stories about the Lipton pound notes began to appear in the newspapers, many of them of the most amusing description. A woman had her purse snatched by a thief and she herself gave chase and assisted to

capture him. At the police court next morning
she was asked how much money there was in the
purse. "Four Lipton pound notes and twopence
in coppers," she told the magistrates solemnly, and
she couldn't understand the shrieks of laughter
which her statement evoked.

One afternoon, I was driving through Dumbar-
ton with some friends when, in a traffic hold-up, a
tramp came up, begging. Jocularly, I offered him
one of my "own" pound notes. This he greedily
seized and disappeared before I could throw him
a copper or two. Next day I read in the papers
that a vagrant had been up before the local magistrate and sentenced for trying to pass a Lipton
pound in exchange for a glass of beer at a public-
house. This incident also helped to bring home to
me the dangers of my latest form of publicity. In
addition, respectable people everywhere began to
be looked at askance the minute they proffered a
pound note under any circumstances whatever!
To say the least of it, it must have been disconcert-
ing to decent citizens to have their money peered
at and most carefully examined before they were
given change for perfectly legal pound notes.

But perhaps the best story in this connection
was never made public although I have told it
repeatedly in private. The most popular music-
hall in these days was the old Scotia. Near by
was a public bar known as Shelley's and here all
the professionals were wont to gather after the

SIR THOMAS'S WORLD-FAMOUS STEAM YACHT *ERIN*

performance was over of an evening. To the bar also came all the young bloods of the town with theatrical leanings. One night at Shelley's a very popular and generally cheery comedian was found to be in the blackest of moods. Urged to dispel his melancholy in the flowing-bowl the comedian rolled out a most tragic story about domestic misfortunes, lack of engagements, etc., and ended up by saying dramatically that his career was ended, finished, blasted—and all for the sake of a few pounds! The generous heart of young Glasgow was touched. Somebody suggested a whip-round with the hat. "Here's a pound to start with!" said one. "And here's another!" chimed in his neighbour. The comedian could scarcely believe his eyes or his ears when, a few minutes later, he found himself the recipient of thirty-five pounds, one shilling and fourpence—the odd money all in coppers.

"Why, this is the most wonderful testimonial I have ever received in my professional life!" exclaimed the overjoyed comedian. "Every man-jack in the bar must now have a drink with me. Give it a name, boys, and don't stint yourselves. Glasgow for ever!"

It was not until next morning that the unlucky comedian discovered that every one of the thirty-five "pounds" was a Lipton note! He came up to my headquarters in such great distress that I was moved to console him with a few real notes, and even these he examined most carefully before taking his departure. As a matter of fact, by this time I was becoming fed up with the "stunt", and began to do my utmost to withdraw the Lipton notes from "circulation". I was hastened in this endeavour by an action being brought against my firm in the Small Debt Court for the sum of one pound—"the amount of loss sustained by pursuer in consequence of having inadvertently taken in change handed to him at a bookstall one of Lipton's Pound Notes". Judgment was given in my favour because the judge held that "a mere moment's examination would have proved to any intelligent person that the note was only an advertisement".

"Only an advertisement!" Yes, but what an advertisement! I have never been able to compute its value in the building up and consolidation of my business.

The Lipton "bank-notes" having served their purpose I waited a few months before hitting the public with something else. All this time I was a very large user of space in the daily, evening and weekly papers. This form of publicity cannot be improved upon for sustained effectiveness—I thought so fifty years ago and I still think so to-day—but if you can back it up with a practical novelty, particularly one that will make the people laugh, you have solved the problem of complete and successful advertising.

My next surprise was the Lipton Mirrors. One was a convex and the other a concave and both were fitted up at the entrances to my various shops. The one marked "Going to Lipton's" showed the faces of all who looked into it elongated and miserable to the extent of a couple of yards. The other, entitled "Coming from Lipton's", puffed everybody out to an enormous girth and made the faces round, jolly and care-free. These mirrors were a sensation for months. Millions of people must have looked into them, children came from far and near to enjoy the free novelty and there was more spontaneous laughter outside and inside my shops than in any music-hall or theatre in the town. Once more originality and enterprise reflected themselves immediately and conspicuously in my turn-over.

There are many ways in which I worked this "going to" and "coming from" idea. Apart from having it in cartoons and drawings for my windows and for newspaper advertisements I played it up on the streets of all the cities where I had branches. At one time I would employ perhaps a dozen of the most "buxomest" women I could find, dress them all in the same style and provide them with baskets on which were written the words: "I'm bound for Lipton's". A procession of these plump ladies, walking along the side-path in single file and smiling most genially as if engaged in a delightful task seldom failed to attract tremendous attention.

Another angle to this idea was to hire a crew of the slimmest and most cadaverous males that could be collected in any town or city and have them walk up one side of the street. They were each ticketed "Going to Lipton's". Parading along the other side was an equal number of the fattest and best-fed and jolliest-looking fellows we were able to lay hands upon and they were all "Coming from Lipton's"!

In 1881—I give the exact year because there have been scores and scores of arguments about it ever since—I pulled off what was admitted to be the cleverest piece of advertising which had been successfully attempted by any British trader. I had only three shops at the time and was exceedingly keen on having a real big Christmas attraction for them—something which would make the people of Glasgow literally sit up and take notice. I wracked my brains over this puzzle for many weeks but the inspiration wouldn't come. It had to be a rip-snorter—or nothing at all. Then all at once, when serving a customer one afternoon with a two-pound slice of cheese, the idea came to me that I would import, display, and sell, the largest cheese ever made in the world. There was only one place to get this cheese—America. And even in America there was only one man who I knew could make it —Dr. L. L. Wright, of Whiteborough, New York. The cables were set humming at once. Within a few hours of the idea being conceived every detail was fixed and I knew that six weeks before Christmas my monster cheese would arrive at Glasgow from New York.

Naturally I got very busy on preliminary announcements. I advertised the name of the ship on which the cheese was coming across the Atlantic, I advertised the day and hour of her arrival, I advertised the fact that eight hundred cows had given their entire milk for six days to allow of the record cheese being made and that two hundred dairymaids had been kept busy over the same period, that the world's best cheese experts had been in consultation so that Lipton's customers might partake of the largest and finest cheese ever made in human history! There were actually hundreds of people at the Broomielaw when the steamer did arrive and many thousands more assembled in the main streets of the city to see the Giant Cheese— "Jumbo" was its name—conveyed from the docks by steam traction-engine to my principal store. A Royal Visit could hardly have roused more enthusiasm. The Procession of the Cheese was an event which was spoken of for many a day afterwards in Glasgow. We had the utmost difficulty in getting the cheese into the main window of the shop but when we did finally have it "posed" in all its massive grandeur it was an object of admiration and awe to daily crowds for several weeks.

"Jumbo, the Giant Cheese" having been safely ensconced in the largest window of my largest shop,

and having created a sensation throughout the West
of Scotland, I went home to my father and mother
feeling that I had accomplished something out of
the ordinary even for a progressive young shopkeeper with ideas behind him. I told them all about
the Cheese and how much I was hoping the advertisement would be a good advertisement for the
business. With her usual fine judgment my mother
remarked :

"It will be a better advertisement still, Tom, if
the cheese is a good cheese!"

Here, of course, my dear mother unconsciously
put her finger on one of the elemental principles
of sound business and of advertising. All the
publicity in the world will not establish the sale of
a bad article. All the advertisement "lay-outs"
that genius ever invented with the express object
of tempting customers to buy will fail lamentably
if the goods fall short of the "boost".

Already I had begun to realize this vital thing in
my own business but my mother's quiet observation that night sank into my brain and I never forgot it for the rest of my life. It confirmed, if con-
firmation were necessary, my determination to give
the public who patronized my stores the very best
quality of goods that my money could purchase in
the first instance or theirs, over my counters, in the
second.

Fortunately I was able to assure my mother that
"Jumbo" was a cheese of unassailable reputation

for I had already tested it myself with every possible satisfaction. And then the idea came to me: why not make the Giant Cheese "a better advertisement still" by turning it into a Golden Cheese by the simple method of hiding a large quantity of sovereigns or half-sovereigns in its vast interior? By carrying this into effect I scored a big hit. Indeed, I never expected anything like the public excitement it created.

When the cheese came to be cut up and sold on Christmas Eve, I had certainly expected a large crowd and had arranged with the police authorities for a dozen officers to be present for the ostensible purpose of keeping order, although, to tell the truth, this was more of an advertising dodge than anything else. As it transpired a hundred policemen would not have been too many, for the street was stormed by a vast concourse of people from all over the city anxious to have a "dip" into Lipton's golden cheese. Prompt to the minute announced I started to cut up "Jumbo". The excitement was intense. In four pound, three pound, two pound and even half-pound portions the cheese melted, "like sna' aff a dyke" as we say in Scotland, and in less than two hours "Jumbo" was no more.

Many of the purchasers could not restrain their impatience to find out if they had "struck lucky". Immediately they received their parcels from my assistants they tore the paper off and began to explore their portions, some of them doing this even before they had left the counter. Others, clamorous to be served themselves, pulled and elbowed them out of the way. Groans from the disappointed ones mixed with shouts of glee from those who were fortunate. As often as not both types struggled back to the counter for "another cut". Pandemonium reigned—but it was a laughing, perfectly good-natured pandemonium and the merriment was increased all round when it was discovered that even the policemen sent to maintain order had themselves yielded to temptation and were lining up alongside for as large chunks of "Jumbo" as they could afford to buy. One policeman found a sovereign in his portion as he was half-way to the door and he was so overjoyed that he started dancing a fandango in the course of which he lost his helmet! Hundreds of would-be customers never got inside the doors. Had "Jumbo" been five times its size I could have sold every ounce that Christmas Eve. Of course, the newspaper reporters came along in force and next morning I had columns of free publicity.

CHAPTER X

CONVINCED that I had got hold of a really good idea in this Giant Cheese stunt, and equally satis- fied that it could be carried on, with necessary embellishments, for a long time in different parts of the country I made arrangements with an American company to instal special machinery for the manufacture of still larger cheeses—so large that several of them weighed five tons each. To pro- duce the largest of them, thirty-five tons of milk were used. Another required the milk of four thousand cows.

Circumstances generally combined to aid me in making my Christmas "displays" of the cheeses a success. Arriving in Nottingham one morning, I found my manager wondering how he was going to have his three-ton cheese removed from the station. In his dilemma he asked my advice.

"There's a circus in the town, isn't there?" I remarked. (I had seen it myself on the way from the station to the shop.) "Well, what about getting me one of the elephants to draw the cheese from the goods yard to the shop, going by way of all the principal street? It will be a first-class stunt as the Yankees say!"

And it *was*. Nottingham turned out to the last man to see the procession. The services of the elephant cost us thirty shillings—just about the cheapest transport in the books of the branch for that year, considering the advertisement.

The cutting up of the cheese was now such a huge business that, to add a still further note of comedy to my Christmas show, I invited contractors to tender for the work, as though it were a big engineering feat. And in Edinburgh, the masses felt assured of some sport for an officially-worded announcement was issued to the effect that, "after careful consideration of the many tenders received for the cutting up of the 'Jumbo' Cheese on Christmas Eve the firm had decided to accept that of a hundred students from the University".

With high-spirited, hot-blooded youth at the prow of the cheese-cutting, a rag seemed certain. Naturally the students were out for fun, but I, too, determined that the fun should not be all on their side. So, when a large number of bright youths crowded into the main window, the glass panes from which had been removed, they found themselves up against an impossible task. The huge cheese was to be cut by a wire at which they pulled in vain. Try as they would, they could make no impression and not one of them realized that the

SIR THOMAS LIPTON, SIR HARRY LAUDER, AND COLONEL WALTER
SCOTT, OF NEW YORK, PHOTOGRAPHED ON THE STAGE OF
A PHILADELPHIA THEATRE

obstacle which prevented their doing so was a great iron-bar against which "Jumbo" was resting. It was only when an artful shopman slyly took this away that the wire sank properly into the cheese. And such was the force of the impact that the yelling, laughing, puffing students lost their grip and were sent sprawling through the window to the tune of loud cheers from the onlooking crowd.

At Sunderland the police authorities objected to the selling of the monster cheese on the score that as it contained sovereigns the transaction became of the nature of a lottery. And lotteries were not allowed in the law-abiding town of Sunderland. I found I could keep within the arm of the law, however, if I sold the cheese having first warned the public that they must return all money found in the cheese to my local manager. So, I inserted a facetious advertisement in the local papers to this effect. We sold every ounce of the cheese in double-quick time, and, of course, not one half-sovereign was ever returned!

Practically the same thing happened at Newcastle, only here the police objection was that the lives of the populace might be endangered through swallowing sovereigns unawares! So I warned the Newcastle public by prominent advertisements in the local papers, that any man or woman buying a portion of the Giant Cheese at Lipton's Christmas Market, stood in very grave danger of being choked by the large number of sovereigns with

which the cheese was liberally sprinkled throughout. I headed this announcement *Police Warning,*
and people rolled up in their thousands, eager to
be choked. And I never heard that anybody was!

No matter how popular an advertisement device
or scheme may be it has been my invariable
experience that its effectiveness must wane in course
of time unless a spice of novelty is continually
being thrown in. So in later years I used to engage
people prominently in the public eye at the moment
to preside at the ceremony of cutting up the cheeses.
I never managed to pull off a Scottish Lord Provost
but I roped in a good few English and Irish
mayors. A popular comedian was always a sure
touch and had my great friend, Harry Lauder,
been to the fore in these days I would most
assuredly have offered him a big fee to get into
the window along with the big cheese! Perhaps
he might have done it for nothing—you will note
that I say perhaps!

I believe I was the first advertiser to "use the
air". This was long before the days of the
brothers Wright—those amazing pioneers who
made a Lindbergh possible—and aeroplanes were
undreamed of. But there were balloons. Hearing
that a famous aeronaut was coming to Glasgow to
give an exhibition ascent at a local gala, I promptly
got in touch with him and arranged for one of my
representatives to "go up" in the balloon and dis-
tribute a hundred thousand telegrams from the

clouds extolling the merit of Lipton's bacon and ham, and the purity of his butter. Prizes ranging from twenty pounds in cash down to a flitch of bacon and ten pounds of tea were offered to the first twenty people presenting the "sky telegrams" at the nearest Lipton branch shop—or, for that matter, at any of my shops. Vast crowds watched the ascent and anxiously awaited the competition leaflets to drop from above. Such a scurrying, hither, thither and yonder, as took place when they did begin to fall, borne in a hundred varying directions by the wind, you can well imagine for yourselves. This balloon scheme was so successful in Glasgow that I subsequently tried it out in different parts of the country, including Liverpool, Leicester and Birmingham.

What suits one town or city does not necessarily suit another fifty miles away. I discovered this exceedingly valuable knowledge early in my business life. A hundred pounds spent in a certain way in Peebles, shall we say, may be money thrown in the gutter in Aberdeen—although the mere idea of money in an Aberdeen gutter is perhaps fantastic! Which is to say that I adopted different methods in every town I set out to attack. Always, to begin with, and as a cardinal principle of my business faith, I chose the best shop and the best site I could get hold of, fitted the former up regardless of expense so that it stood out like a jewel from amongst its drab neighbours, and used the local papers to an extent which made me distinctly popular with their advertisement managers. After all that I looked round for my "opening star-turn". At Dublin I appealed to the infectious and light-hearted gaiety of the populace by engaging a newly-married couple to sit for a couple of days in the window and make tea for the customers. At Edinburgh I secured the boisterous assistance of a party of medical students who cut up hams and sliced cheese to the accompaniment of much wit and banter not only amongst the customers but amongst themselves. At Liverpool I showed in the window a magnificent model, carved in butter, of the crack Atlantic liner of the day. Everywhere a different notion was exploited according to the character of the town, its trade, and the tastes and proclivities of the people.

Another advertising proposition which I gave full rein to about this time was the street "procession". One of the most successful processions took place in Glasgow soon after I had entered the tea trade on a large scale. Determined to make a splash in my home town and draw widespread attention to my new activities, I organized secretly a little army of about two hundred men who were ordered to report on a certain morning at my headquarters in Lancefield Street. They hadn't the ghost of an idea what they were wanted for, but they knew the pay would be all right— I may add that in all my stunts I generally paid much more than the usual rates and, of course, got the best service from every person I employed.

On reaching the Lipton headquarters each man was ushered into a large warehouse, cleared for the occasion and transformed into an immense theatrical dressing-room. A couple of hundred Cingalese costumes were all laid out, complete in every detail, and to every few men was attached a competent "dresser" who knew exactly what was required of him, namely, to turn out so many Ceylon "natives", dressed and made-up so that they would have passed muster in the streets of Colombo. Every man carried two little sandwich-boards. One board told the story that "Lipton's Tea is the Finest in the World", and the second announced the fact that it came "Direct from the Tea Gardens to the Tea-Pot". A "squadron" of the biggest and best-looking Cingalese were mounted at the head of the procession. It took Glasgow by storm.

News of the strange "black army" marching through the city spread like wildfire. The streets were lined with spectators and on every hand it was admitted that Lipton had excelled himself in his latest publicity brain-wave. Actually, many of the citizens thought that I had imported the natives from my estates in Ceylon, a splendid testimony to the effective manner in which my dressers had turned out the processionists. At the corner of Argyle Street and Jamaica Street a woman whose husband had been one of my ordinary sandwich-men for several years, and who not unnaturally thought that the black fellows were doing her man out of a good job, tried to create a scene by seizing the bridle of one of the horses and swearing heartily at the man on his back.

"Ye should be ashamed o' yersels, ye black deevils, comin' to Glesca an' daein' honest Scots-men oot o' their jobs!" she yelled as a parting shaft.

"Wheesht, woman, wheesht!" expostulated a friendly policeman, pulling her away from the horse's head. "Them chaps only arrived frae the Indies this mornin' an' canna understaun' a word ye're sayin'. So save yer breath, woman, save yer breath!"

Not until the evening did the lady know that the very man on whom she had poured out the vials of her wrath was her own husband, occupy-ing the proud position of the leader of the Cingalese and chosen for the honour by reason of his ability to play the part! I took good care that the story found its way into the evening papers!

If I say that for a period of at least twenty years practically all my spare time—and the only spare moments I had, it seems to me, must have been those spent in bed, on the train, or on board ship at sea—was devoted to thinking out new and original advertising schemes, I will not be over-shooting the mark. I made a hobby of it. Apart from seeing the Lipton business expand north, south, east, and west, it provided me with all the entertainment I required. The framing-up and the exploitation of a fresh idea kept me mentally invigorated for just so long as the idea worked satisfactorily; when it had fulfilled its purpose and another was required, why, I just went after it hot-foot. Sometimes it came after me!

For instance. On one occasion I was travelling to the East on board the s.s. *Orotava*. In the Red Sea we ran ashore in a mist. As the ship could not be got off, it was decided to jettison some of the cargo. Bales of this and crates of that were brought on deck, and as the sailors started to heave them overboard an idea for a daring and thoroughly original bit of publicity was literally thrust before my eyes. Going down into the engine-room, I tipped one of the engineers—all idle, seeing the ship was hard and fast—to cut me a stencil and provide me with a pot of red paint and a brush. Armed with these I went on deck and, to the vast amusement of the passengers and crew, I painted the words "DRINK LIPTON'S TEA" on as many bales, cases, and crates as I could before they were consigned to the shallow water around the ship. Many of the lighter cases floated ashore all round the coast, and months afterwards I heard of the flotsam and jetsam from the *Orotava* being found by Arabs and other tribes. Whether they had the good sense to follow the advice to drink my tea, I cannot say.

I may add that my light-hearted attempts at advertising my firm in the Red Sea were speedily abandoned when it became apparent that the *Orotava* was in a more hopeless condition than we had at first imagined. Ultimately we had to leave her in the ship's boats and make our way ashore at rather an inhospitable part of the coast. Luckily there was a cable station not very far away, and I was the first man to think of using the station to send a cable to London telling of the mishap to the steamer, but announcing at the same time the safety of the crew and passengers. This cable, signed "Lipton", appeared in every London and provincial paper next morning, and once more I was the "most advertised man in the United Kingdom"—on this occasion without desiring it.

It must have been on my return from this Eastern trip, too, that I got an Egyptian native to help me to cut the word "Lipton" on one of the stones above the entrance to the Great Pyramid. I forgot all about the incident for several years, and it was only brought back to my mind when a Presbyterian minister at Cambuslang, himself just home from a holiday jaunt, solemnly told his flock one Sunday night that their distinguished towns-man, Mr. Lipton, must have had forbears in Pharaoh's land thousands of years ago, for he distinctly saw the name Lipton engraven on one of the great stones of the Sphinx.

Indeed at this period of my business life I would

have been quite prepared to hire the Pyramids altogether and use them as a medium for international advertising, so to speak. I did offer to lease a disused chimney-stack right in the heart of Glasgow, and promised the Corporation to make it a thing of beauty, telling its tale to the world of the excellence of my products. But the Corporation preferred to have the chimney-stack removed rather than accede to my request! I had another bright idea for utilizing all the buoys marking the channel of the Firth of Clyde from Greenock to Glasgow for some such similar purpose, but again my originality was not received with the acclamation I had hoped for from a progressive body like the famous Clyde Trust!

Yet the novelty and appeal of the many advertising methods I let loose in these early years of my career would have been completely evanescent—more, they would utterly have failed—had I deviated by one jot or tittle from the plan I laid down before I served my first customer at Stobcross Street—namely, to sell the best food in the world at the cheapest possible price. I allowed nothing to come between me and that steadfast decision. That I had created, in the short space of a few years, something like a revolution in the provision trade of Scotland and England was freely admitted even by my rivals. But I could not possibly have sold so cheaply as I did had I not, almost from the start, dispensed with the services of the middleman, or wholesale dealer, standing between the merchant and the consumer.

There was, I could plainly see, no room for both the middleman and me in the ham, butter, and egg business if I was going to be in a position to sell these commodities to the public at cheaper rates than they could buy elsewhere. If I paid the middlemen's prices for the provisions I required to retail in my shop, or shops, I would be no better off than any other man trying to make a living by selling the goods in which I specialized. No, I had to forage for my own supplies and sell them at one profit only—my own.

CHAPTER XI

The problem of securing still larger supplies—I turn to Denmark and Sweden—and to the United States—a visit to Chicago in search of pigs.

To get these supplies in the ever-increasing quantity rendered imperative by my constantly developing trade became, not a serious matter, but a very pressing and important one. I started by making regular weekly visits to the north of Ireland and buying from the farmers at their local markets. Later I enlarged the scope of my weekly visits to embrace other districts of Ireland, and I also went to see the farmers and crofters at their own homes and made bargains for taking their entire outputs over a period. By and by I had built up such a reputation amongst the Irish producers that weekly visitation was unnecessary; the postal authorities relieved me of thousands of miles of travel by boat and train and jaunting-car. But even though I was soon able to tell the public that I was in a position to offer them goods "from every county in the Green Isle", it became more and more evident, as time went on, that fresh and liberal sources of supply would have to be found. Literally my Irish friends could not keep pace with the demands of my customers.

In this dilemma I turned to Denmark, Sweden, and Russia, to which Continental countries I dispatched representatives. They carried with them practically open cheque-books. Very soon I was doing a vast turnover with the producers in these countries, and particularly with Denmark, the inhabitants of which seem, from time immemorial, to have been excellent husbandmen, experts in farm produce of all kinds. For the Danes I have always had a great admiration. They can do more with a few acres and a few cows than the farmers of any other nation in the world, with the exception, perhaps, of the Dutch.

My headquarters in Lancefield Street dealt with all the incoming supplies and, of course, their subsequent distribution all over the country. I had my personal office here and, unless when I was away buying or opening new shops, I was on deck from early morning until late at night. A few weeks ago I was speaking to the head of a large London publishing firm, and he amused me by telling me that his father was one of my employees who frequently put in a twelve and fourteen-hour day in the warehouse. On coming home late night after night, the wife would remonstrate with him about the long hours of duty he was putting in, and his usual reply was something like this:

"Why should I complain? I'm gettin' guid wages an' overtime forbye. Besides, a man should never object to workin' for a boss that's in afore him

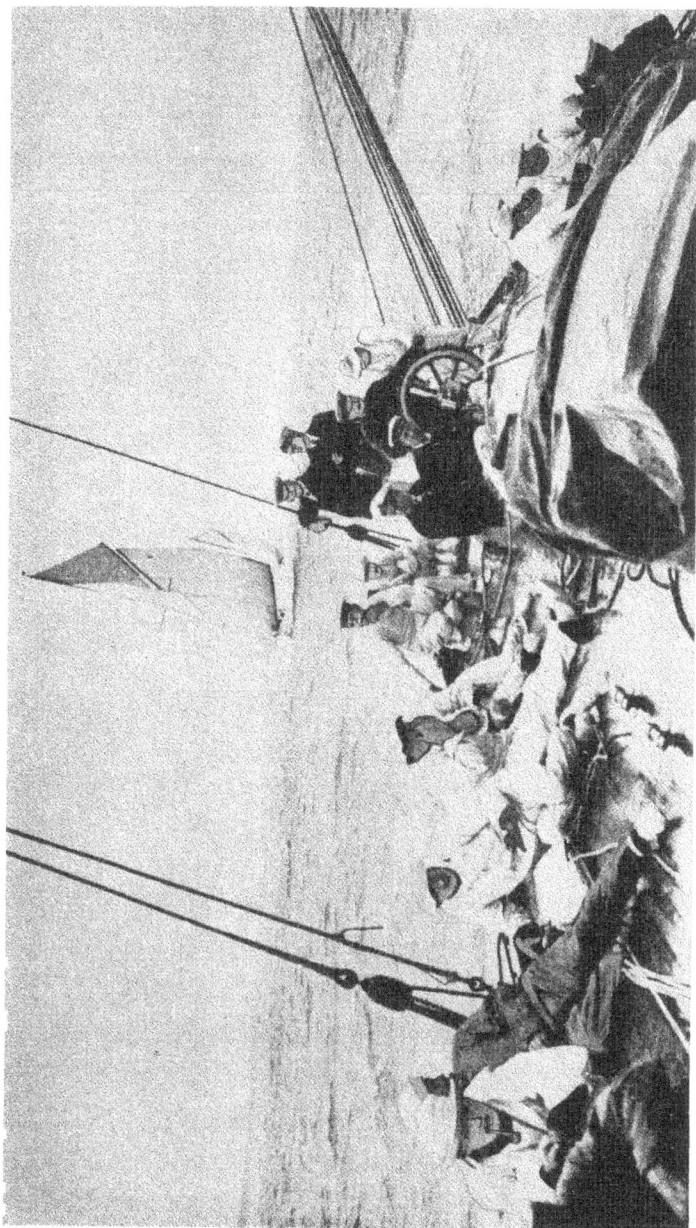

SIR THOMAS LIPTON SEATED BY THE WHEEL OF *SHAMROCK*, SHOWING THE *LULWORTH* AND *WHITE HEATHER* BEHIND DURING COWES REGATTA

1140

in the mornin' an' still busy at it when every other man in the place has gone home!"

As the branch shops multiplied on every point of the compass, the Lancefield Street "base" became more and more important. Extensive alterations and additions had to be made from time to time. Soon it was easily the largest provision "factory" in Scotland. It hummed with activity day and night. The staff was constantly being added to; every day there were new faces—and I welcomed them all with a smile and an encouraging word. I started my own printing works at Lancefield Street and my own paper-bag making department. A few years afterwards the former establishment was printing posters and advertising designs in twenty different languages for dispatch to every corner of the world. This was always a most interesting part of the Lipton headquarters to visitors, and they regarded me with amazement when I told them that I spoke all the languages myself and saw to it that never a mistake was made in the weird and wonderful hieroglyphics of which many of the bills and posters were composed! Actually, of course, expert linguists were employed to keep us right, but I often wondered what my printers and lithographers thought about the millions of quite unintelligible sheets they saw coming pouring out of machines.

But to return to the vital question of supplies. Even with my Continental connections I was finding difficulty in securing the "right stuff at the right price". It was then that my thoughts turned across the Atlantic to the United States. The North American continent was the world's greatest centre for ham, bacon, pork, butter, and cheese. The supply there was practically limitless. Why not, I started to ask myself, bring the products of the far west direct to the consumers of Great Britain and thus save intermediate profits? Better still, why not consider the question of acquiring my own stockyards in the packing district of Chicago and embark on the killing and curing process for myself? I was well aware that there were not at this time—indeed, there never has been—half enough hogs in the whole United Kingdom to supply the home market.

Although I felt certain in my own mind that sooner or later I would be compelled to begin operations in America if my stores kept on increasing at the rate they were doing, it was not until after I had carried out an experiment that I decided definitely to make my second trip to the United States. This experiment took the shape of sending a young man in my employment across the Atlantic to buy butter and cheese. He was a bright Irish youth of an enterprising nature, and my confidence in him was not misplaced, for he achieved all the success I had anticipated for the scheme. By having a representative on the spot, I found I was able to buy butter and cheese at such prices that I could pass on the advantage to my customers—in other words, I was in a position to sell these articles at prices hitherto unknown in Britain. At seven o'clock one evening I made up my mind.

"Mother," I announced just as we all sat down to supper, "I'm off to America to-morrow. You must help me pack to-night!" This news was a bit of a bombshell, but the best of all mothers in the world was soon busying herself looking out my clothes (and no evening dress was included in *that* outfit, let me tell you!), laying aside socks, collars, ties, and "mufflers", and all the while overflowing with advice and counsel as to my health, food, and habits (with particular warning never to sleep in a damp bed!) while on my travels.

This second trip of mine to America was an important landmark in my business career. Indeed, I often think that it had a distinct bearing on my whole future. It was the precursor of many, many visits over a long period of years, and it implanted in my heart a genuine affection for the American people which I have never attempted to conceal and which has gone on increasing with the passage of time. It is no bad compliment to my own land to say that for fifty years I have been as much at home in the United States and among their peoples as I have felt in the bosom of "ma ain kith an' kin". Somehow, America has never seemed to me to be a strange country; certainly from the moment I set foot in New York as a boy, I don't think I ever once experienced the sensation of being on a "foreign strand". Probably this was owing to the fact that at the outset of my American associations I became a strong admirer of the spirit of genial combativeness which is so essential a feature of the average American man—of the "go-get-it" determination which stamps Americanism all the way through. I felt, rightly or wrongly, that I had in me a dash of the American character.

On this occasion of my second visit the conditions were, of course, greatly changed. I had money in my pocket. I was independent. Now I had come, not to see what I could humbly offer to America, but what America could offer me, a young business man anxious to spend his money to the best advantage. And let me say at once that I enjoyed every minute of the six weeks to which my trip extended. I was still, to all intents and purposes, an unknown individual, but I was received everywhere with a hearty handshake and a warm kindliness. The few people I did know, through having had business dealings with them by correspondence, went miles out of their way to help me in carrying out my schemes and ideas.

In view of the nature of these, Chicago was my main objective, and I lost as little time as possible in arriving at the great city on Lake Michigan. At once I set myself to find out all I could about the packing industry, then, as now, the main occupation of the majority of its citizens. For a few days I did a bit of quiet scouting on my own, making judicious inquiries here and there and keeping my eyes open for wrinkles and suggestions. I also visited all the big stockyards, and at these I was so inquisitive that the guides and other employees must have thought I was the most keenly interested stranger they had ever seen on the premises. I was.

At length, I found myself in possession of just what I wanted—a building with the facilities for killing and dressing 300 to 400 pigs a day. I "hustled some" to have the factory in going order, and when it did open its doors under the title of the Cork Packing House, I had the feeling that my enterprise had been very much worth while. Here I would like to pay a tribute to the courtesy and goodwill extended to me at this crucial time in my life by my competitors in the pork-packing trade. Men of such weight and position as P. D. Armour, Louis Swift, Nelson Morris, John Hately, and T. C. Boyd showed me immense kindness, and the assistance they gave me kept me from making many blunders in a branch of business absolutely new to me and, as may well be imagined, studded with pitfalls for the unwary new-comer.

In addition to the men I have mentioned, I was fortunate in having the good-natured help of the well-known firm of Kingan & Co. By a happy chance the principal partners of this company hailed from Belfast, and they remembered me from the days when I used to make my weekly trips to Ireland to buy the butter, eggs, and cheese with which to stock my first little shop in Stobcross Street. Having known me at my start, they could hardly credit that I had now between thirty and forty shops and was selling more goods than any individual firm in Scotland or England. They provided me, in Mr. John McNeill, with my first Chicago manager, and they also initiated me into the secret of a special process for the curing of hogs which made the resultant bacon and hams impervious to climatic conditions all over the world. The friendly spirit manifested towards me at this time in Chicago left a very lasting impression on my mind; and I think I must have made a favourable hit with the Chicago pork-packers themselves, for many years later the daughter of one of their number told me that her father used to refer to my arrival amongst them in the stockyards somewhat in this fashion:

"Do I remember Tommy Lipton sitting-in at the pork-packing game in Chicago? I'll say I do. Till I met him, I always thought that your Britisher was slow to get a move on at anything, but this Lipton guy quickly knocked *that* notion for nix. Why, he just shooted around like an express train so that none of us ever saw him for more'n ten seconds at one time!"

This description of my personality and methods in these days amused me very much. It was, of course, too flattering altogether, but it was a typical American "I'll-hand-it" tribute to a business competitor from over the sea.

CHAPTER XII

My first real holiday in America—a surprise encounter with President Hayes—I meet the confidence tricksters and succeed in handing them over to the police in Washington—a "special" train for two to Montreal in search of cheese.

WHEN, ten days or a fortnight after my arrival in Chicago, I had the Cork Packing House in full blast, I decided to have a holiday—the first luxury of the kind I had ever allowed myself in my life thus far. I had seen a good deal of the Eastern and Southern States as a boy working my way round from place to place, but the conditions were now much more in my favour. I could pick and choose my centres for visitation. Naturally the first place I selected was Washington. And I hadn't been in the famous capital many hours before I shook hands with President Hayes! I wonder how many Englishmen, before or since, have beaten my record for a quick line-up alongside an American President.

Here is the story. Having learned at the hotel that Mr. Hayes held frequent receptions which were open to all and sundry—a piece of information not strictly correct, perhaps, but one which interested me immensely—and that, in fact, this particular day was a reception day, I promptly hired a cab and drove up to the historic residence which stands second only in my eyes to Buckingham Palace itself.

There was not a soul in sight when I got to the front door, but I boldly rang the bell, nevertheless. In answer to my summons a manservant appeared, and I asked him quietly if the President was at home.

"He is, sir!" replied the servant. "Will you please follow me?"

Feeling just a wee bit nervous by the total absence of the crowds I had expected to mix with on an official reception day, I did as I was bid and was duly shown into a spacious room on the first floor. It was tenanted by one single gentleman, very amiable in aspect, whom I took to be a private secretary or, at least, an important clerk. He came forward at once and warmly shook me by the hand. I felt at home on the instant, and we commenced to talk in the freest and friendliest manner. On my announcing that I came from Scotland, the gentleman expressed his delight and inquired if I happened to know some of his cousins who lived in the Fair City of Perth. He was just about to tell me the family name of his cousins when I broke in with the information that I didn't know Perth, but that I fully intended to open a shop there when I went home. In this way we chatted on various subjects for fully twenty minutes. I got to like him so much and was so thoroughly enjoying his brilliant conversation that I decided to ask him to lunch, and did so in these words:

"Sir, I would appreciate the pleasure of your company to lunch in my hotel after I have had the honour of meeting the President. Can you tell me when the reception is likely to begin to-day?"

My friend looked at me quizzically. "But I am President Hayes!" he quietly observed.

I was aghast at my blunder and offered profuse apologies, but the genial President of the United States broke out into hearty laughter, and it was not until later we learned that I had been mistaken for a visitor who had an official appointment with the First Citizen and had been ushered without further ceremony into his august presence! Can you wonder at it that all my life I have had a supreme regard for President Hayes and for all the distinguished men who have succeeded him in his illustrious office?

An adventure of a totally different kind befell me two days later. Moving around Washington and admiring the sights of that beautiful city—beautiful even in these far-off days, but incomparable to-day —I was hailed by an extremely well-dressed and attractively-spoken young man who slapped me on the shoulder, laughed gleefully over what was to him an unexpected and pleasant meeting, and went on to ask me "why on earth I hadn't written to let him know I was coming to Washington?"

I explained that I was a complete stranger from overseas and that he must be labouring under a delusion. Still, I added, there was no harm done; mistakes of identity were not uncommon.

"Say, if you're not Henry Edwards, of Indianapolis, you must be his twin brother!" ejaculated the young man, staring at me as if he had seen a ghost. "And if you're not that, it just licks creation. I'm real sorry, sir, if I've made a mistake, and I ask your pardon!"

Of course, after that we fell to talking, and a few minutes later we were strolling around the city as if we had been friends for years. Together we visited the House of Representatives, and I found my companion to be a walking mine of knowledge. He knew everything and everybody. I was thoroughly delighted with his wit, wisdom, and charming courtesy. On coming out of the House a distinguished-looking man passed us and nodded agreeably to my companion. Then his eyes fell upon me and, to my unbounded amazement, he also hailed me as Henry Edwards and proceeded to ask me when I had arrived from Indianapolis. Explanations followed, and the new-comer—whom my first friend addressed as "Colonel" one moment and "George" the next—could scarcely get over his conviction that I was indeed Henry Edwards and that we were having a game with him. By and by it was mutually agreed that Thomas Lipton, of Glasgow, Scotland, had in Henry Edwards, of Indianapolis, State of Indiana, the most lifelike replica in the history of mankind.

SIR THOMAS LIPTON IN THE UNIFORM OF HIS MAJESTY'S
LIEUTENANCY OF THE CITY OF LONDON

Do you begin to get the idea? Of course you do. But I must confess that I did not—at least, until it was almost too late!

The remainder of the story takes its well-known and justly famous course. The "Colonel" could not stay long with us; he had an invitation to attend the unveiling of a statue on the outskirts of Washington, across the Potomac, and the occasion was to be a big public ceremony with the subsequent rejoicings taken part in by "Red Cloud" and "Spotted Tail", two Indian chiefs whose exploits were then on everybody's lips. Ha! come to think of it, he had two tickets for the reserved enclosure —would I not come with him as his guest? Very, very kind of him, but I could not possibly leave my first friend who had been so kind to me. The name of the latter, by the way, was "Charlie", and he was palpably pleased at my decision to remain with him. "All right! All right! Must be off now," says the "Colonel". Hopes to see Charlie later in the day and is truly delighted at having made my acquaintance. If ever he is in Glasgow he'll sure look me up. And, all smiles and breathing good fellowship, the breezy "Colonel" rushes off!

An hour later we are overjoyed to run into him again. He explains that one of the Senators had kept him busy on important affairs of state, but that he has managed to hire a special boat to row him over the Potomac so as to be in time for the ceremony. Also, by a bit of great good luck, he got another ticket for the unveiling; he could now take both of us and would brook no denial. Personally, I am delighted. I am still young enough to be very keenly interested, not so much in the statue, but in the prospect of seeing "Red Cloud" and "Spotted Tail". So we all hurry to the riverside and are rowed across in a boat by a burly negro who is constantly urged by the "Colonel" to put pep into his work at the oars. We land at a deserted spot, the negro goes off with his boat and we hurry forward for the better part of a mile into the country—which, by the way, becomes more and more desolate the farther we go. At last we run into a disgruntled-faced man coming in our direction.

"Say," he greets us without further preliminary, "if you guys is goin' to see the unveilin' o' the statue you may as well save your wind. The ceremony's been postponed at the last minute an' thousands o' folks like myself have been turned away. Ain't it jes' too bad now!"

That remark about the "thousands of folks" woke me up from my dream. There didn't seem to be another soul within two miles of the four of us. I saw the whole thing clearly. But not by the flicker of an eyelid did I convey my feelings either to the "Colonel", to "Charlie", or to the stranger who had introduced himself to us as a horse-dealer from Kentucky, and who had been "clean tickled to death" at the idea of seeing "Red Cloud" and

"Spotted Tail" doing their famous stunts. In due course the confederacy got very busy. They were clearly delighted at my complete lack of suspicion and more than delighted at my readiness to try my hand at a game of "Monte". Of course, one of the trio—the "Colonel" as it happened—gave me a solemn wink and urged me in a whisper not to risk too much at first.

"Even if I lose all I've got with me it won't hurt me," said I jovially, at the same moment turning both my trouser pockets outside in and exposing the huge sum of eleven dollars and thirty-three cents. I shall never forget the blank looks of baffled disappointment on the faces of the rogues; likewise, I shall never forget how frightened I was they would "go through me" and find the thousand dollars odd which I had secretly stowed away in an invisible breast-pocket stitched in the lining of my waistcoat. To prevent anything like the latter happening I strongly urged that I was a keen card-player, that I had plenty of money at the hotel and that I should be allowed to go back to Washington for my "roll" so that I could show them I was as good a sportsman as any of them. This sugges-tion of mine intrigued the others.

"But what's goin' to prevent you leavin' us cold an' never comin' back?" asked the horse-dealer from Kentucky gloomily. To this I replied that I should never dream of such a thing; I was enjoy-ing myself too much and, besides, the "Colonel"

and "Charlie" were my best friends in America
from whom I was determined on no account to be
severed. Indeed, I added, why should not the
"Colonel" come back with me to the hotel where
I had fully ten thousand dollars locked up in my
travelling-case?

That did it! The "Colonel" gleefully agreed to
return with me, and the others, no less gleefully,
decided to await our reappearance with the sinews
of war for a "real hot gamble".

The end of the story is obvious. Immediately
my military friend and myself got back to the outskirts of Washington, I left the "Colonel's" side
for a moment on the pretext of hailing a cab, but
instead, walked swiftly up to the first policeman I
saw. The "Colonel" was too quick for us, however, and bolted, and I never saw him or "Charlie"
or the horse-dealer again! But the Washington
Police laid all three by the heels a few days later.
They proved to be a well-known and successful
gang of confidence men with a long and black list
of offences opposite their names. Found guilty,
they went for "a stretch", and a few days later I
had the satisfaction of reading all about myself and
the tricksters in a graphic story, displayed across
three columns of the daily Press, bearing the
streamer headlines: "The Three-Card Monte Men.
How the Plan and the Plotters were Neatly Foiled
by a Young Britisher on Holiday".

I had an enjoyable trip after leaving Washington, visiting many places of interest and many cities which had hitherto only been names to me. This tour confirmed me in my affections for America, and in my belief in its great, practically limitless, potentialities as the land of the future. But I had already been too long away from my beloved business across the sea and returned to New York with the intention of getting the first available steamer home. Curiously enough, I had no sooner set foot in dear old Broadway than I ran into a friend who was a cheese-merchant in Montreal with whom I had done business and was anxious to do some more. I told him that I was willing to buy a large quantity of an extra-special kind of cheese which I hadn't so far come across in the States.

"Why, Mr. Lipton," he remarked, "that's funny. I've got what you want in Montreal. Come right up with me and have a look at it. Just the very thing you're after and the price, to you, will be dead right!"

I said it was impossible for me to go north, as the day was Thursday and I was sailing for Liverpool on the Saturday. But my friend pointed out that we could easily travel up that night, spend the day in Montreal, and I could return by the night train on the Friday, arriving in good time for the sailing hour on Saturday. So I decided to make the trip.

In those days there was no dining-car attached to the night trains, and we were informed that there would be a stop for breakfast at Rouse's Point. Sure enough, we were wakened at seven o'clock by the black porter and we hurried over to the restaurant, which was situated, perhaps, a hundred yards or so away from where the train had drawn up. We were the only two passengers ordering breakfast, but we thoroughly enjoyed the meal, and at the end of a quarter of an hour we started to make tracks for the train again. To our blank amazement, however, it had gone on to Montreal without us. My friend was tremendously upset. There wouldn't be another train for many hours; in any case it was pretty certain that I could not now arrive in Montreal in time to catch the early night train back to New York the same evening. The only thing left for me would be to wait at Rouse's Point for the first south-going train.

"Not a bit of it," I argued. "I intend going to Montreal by hook or by crook. And when I set out to do anything I generally do it. Leave this to me."

My friend's expression plainly conveyed that he did not think I could do much, but he agreed to my suggestion. So I proceeded to find the station-master who, I soon discovered, was unaware that we were two passengers left behind by the train which had just departed a few minutes earlier, and I thought it better not to inform him of this fact. He politely asked what he could do for us.

"We want to go to Montreal as quickly as possible," I explained. "When is the next train?"

"Why, there's one just gone," he replied. "Usually this train stops here for twenty minutes for breakfast but this morning, for some reason or another, we got orders for it to go right through to the junction at St. John's for the breakfast stop."

"Couldn't I get a special train?" I asked.

The station-master looked us both up and down critically. We didn't look like the type of men who would run to "specials"; and in a half-hearted way he replied that he reckoned we could but it would cost us a hundred and fifty dollars.

"Very reasonable, indeed," I remarked, nudging my friend hard to prevent him from interfering. This observation of mine altered the station-master's outlook at once. He began to hustle. He telegraphed to headquarters and got permission to run a special to Montreal. Then he telegraphed to the junction at St. John's and found a goods engine there with steam up. There was a spare coach at his own depot. In less than half an hour our "special" was ready. I went up to the engine-driver and told him that I would see him right if he got us to Montreal in good time.

"Say, boss," smiled that worthy. "You don't need to recognize me at Montreal if this old engine don't move some!"

Thereafter, for the first time in my life—but by no means for the last—I stepped aboard my own special train. The conductor put chairs on the rear platform, tested the ice-water tank, and saw that the fans were in working order. The engine-driver held to his promise, and we swept along at a terrific rate. I felt for all the world like a Governor-General travelling in state. But my friend was gloomy and miserable. The thought of the hundred and fifty dollars was evidently worrying him so much that he paid little attention to the garrulous descriptions of the places we were passing provided by the talkative conductor. So far as I was concerned, these helped to enliven the journey.

As we approached Montreal the conductor suavely expressed the hope that we had enjoyed the trip.

"Splendid," said I.

"Everything to your satisfaction?" he went on.

"Magnificent!" said I.

"That's real fine," said the conductor. "Now, sir, if you please, I'll collect the hundred and fifty dollars."

"Is this Montreal we are coming to?" I asked.

"Sure thing, sir," said the conductor.

"Well," I replied. "Montreal is the place I bought our tickets for and here they are!"—handing over the ordinary tickets I had bought at New York.

The conductor's face was a study. Then he commenced to laugh.

"That's a good joke," said he.

"There's no joke about it," said I. "That is, unless you have taken us to some other place than Montreal and then the joke would be on you!"

"This is Montreal and you must settle up or go with me to the manager's office," announced the conductor, now rather convinced that he was up against some trouble.

So, on our arrival, to the manager's office we went. There, the conductor explained that I had ordered a special train from Rouse's Point and now refused to pay for it.

"Excuse me," I said. "All that I told the station-master there was that a hundred and fifty dollars was very reasonable for a special train. I paid for two tickets at New York for Montreal and here they are! When I purchased the tickets I was told by one of your officials that there would be a stop of twenty minutes at Rouse's Point. There wasn't, and the train went off without us."

At first the manager thought I was joking. Then I explained to him that we should have had twenty minutes for breakfast at Rouse's Point, that we only took fifteen minutes and then found the train had gone. The porter of the sleeping-car was sent for and confirmed my story. The conductor of the train had forgotten to tell the porter of the changed orders, and the porter had forgotten that we were at breakfast. The manager apologized. "But," said he, "I must, of course, ask you to pay for the special train, and I will give you my word that the amount will be refunded to you."

"There's nothing in this world," said I, "I'd rather do. But how can I? I've only got three dollars—you're welcome to that if you want it. Here's my ticket. If this is Montreal, why should I pay more?"

The upshot was that I was fired out of that office. I went to my friend's store, saw his cheese, and caught the train back for New York that afternoon. I noticed several people looking at me curiously. Presently a Yankee drummer came up.

"Pardon me, stranger," he asked, "but are you the long fellow who rolled into Montreal this morning in such almighty fine style on a special train?"

"The same fellow," I replied smilingly.

"Wall, put it right there!" He extended his hand as he said the words. "You're the first man on this planet who ever got the better of the Canadian railroads! I am going to New York myself," he went on, "and you can have anything you darn well like on the way at my expense." We noticed during the journey that whenever the train stopped and my new friend and I went to the refreshment rooms for something to eat or drink, we found on either side of us the conductor and

the brakesman of the train and on our asking them
how it was that their appetites seemed to keep pace
with ours they replied: "We have been given strict
orders never to let that long fellow out of our sight,
as if we did we would find him arriving at New
York on a special train."

CHAPTER XIII

Home again—opening new shops all over the King-dom—I enter the tea trade, with amazing results—the intricacies of blending—competition in Mincing Lane.

INVIGORATED and inspired by my holiday in America, I threw myself with greater energy than before into the still further extension of my business on returning home. Things had gone well in my absence, a fact which pleased me exceedingly because it proved that I had been building on the right lines and that my judgment of colleagues and assistants and work-people had been justified. There is, I always think, something wrong in any business or organization which is absolutely dependent on one man, or, for that matter, on two or three men. The foundation of a business can generally be traced to the determination, the vision, the genius—call it what you will—of one man in particular, but the conduct of that business, after it has been successfully launched and its guiding principles firmly established, should not depend for its smooth running upon the personality of a single individual. The biggest and most prosperous business in the world are those in which the chief executive positions are held by men who have grown up with the organizations, who have been trained and confirmed in their methods and their ideals, and who themselves are capable of handling the practical details, if need be, from the bottom to the top of the outfit.

I now concentrated on the opening of many more new shops all over the Kingdom. Seldom a week elapsed without a new Lipton branch opening its doors. And every one started without a penny of debt. All the profits of the business went straight back into the business. I realized that I could not have my cake and eat it. My own personal expenditure remained on a very modest scale. It is true that as I prospered it was my pride and joy to see that my mother and father had a bit more comfort, even luxury, but for myself my wants continued to be few. If I got enough to eat and a nice bed to rest in for six out of the twenty-four hours I was well content. The "game of business" was always much more to me than the financial results of the game, but it would be stupid on my part to deny that the knowledge of my firm's rapid and successful expansion was at once delightful and exhilarating. Here was all the excitement, all the romance, all the encouragement, and—if you insist—all the literal "rewards" which I required to make my strenuous life happy.

By this time, say about the years 1884-7, I had gathered round me a thoroughly competent group of managers, buyers, cashiers and accountants, to say nothing of the rank and file. I even had my

own architect and solicitor—two most valuable
aides-de-camp considering the large number of new
shops I was buying or leasing and the very large
amount of technical and legal details involved in
the various transactions. These things I could
never have carried out by myself. The architect
and the solicitor and myself spent a great part of
our lives in express trains careering all over the
land; indeed, it became a standing joke with these
two gentlemen that they seldom knew in which
city of Great Britain they were going to sleep on
any particular night. But I, myself, moved round
even more. In one week, I remember, I put in a
full working day at each of the following, widely-
separated towns : Aberdeen, Glasgow, Belfast,
Newcastle and Manchester, every night being
passed in trains or in the bunks of cross-channel
steamboats !

Looking back now, and endeavouring to mark
off in stages my business career as, perhaps, the
world's largest individual merchant, I should say
that the years between 1888 and 1898 were easily
the most important. For one thing they found
me definitely established in the tea-trade and for
another these ten years saw the Lipton organization expand tremendously not only in Great
Britain but in many different parts of the world.
My name has become so inextricably associated
with the merchandising of tea in the minds of nine
out of every ten persons that I feel I must make

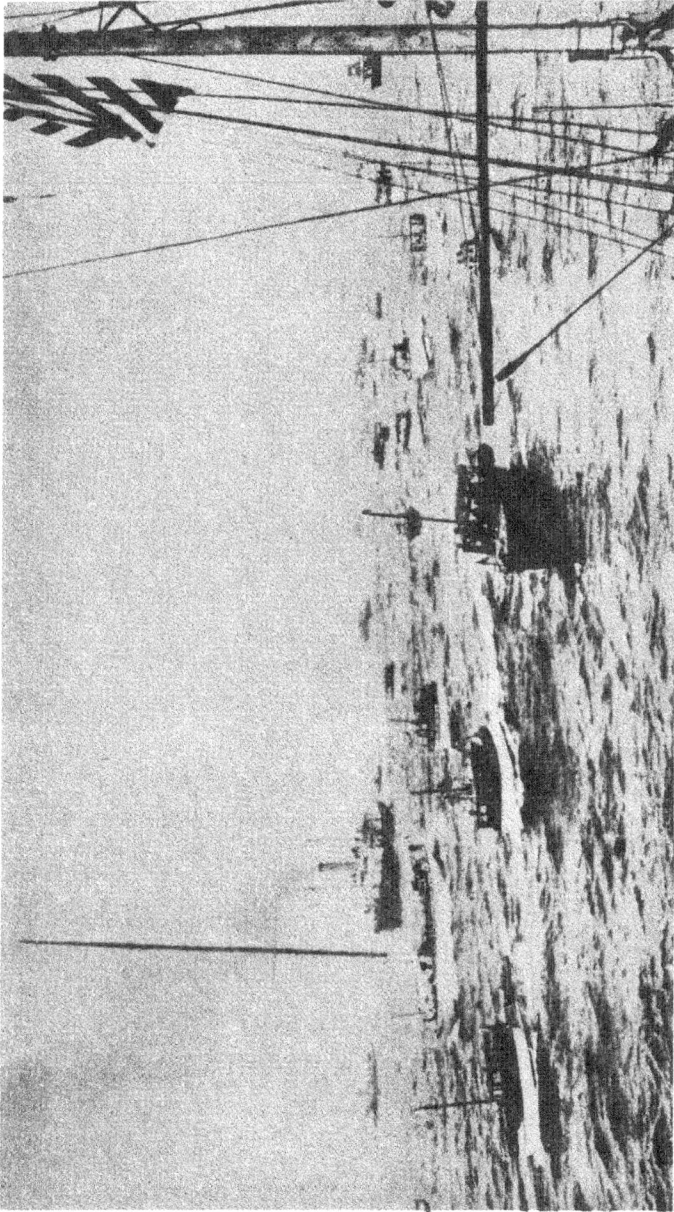

WATERCRAFT OF EVERY DESCRIPTION FOLLOWING IN THE WAKE OF THE GREAT RACE BETWEEN *ENTERPRISE* AND *SHAMROCK V*

[*Topical Press*]

this point clear—my entry into the tea business only took place after I had more or less achieved all I originally set out to do in the general provision trade. Not till then did I begin to see the tremendous possibilities of tea as an adjunct to the other commodities in which I was dealing.

The drinking of tea had become very much more general in Britain during the late 'eighties. As a beverage it might be said to have come into its own during the same years in which I was building up the "Lipton Markets". The wholesale tea merchants were not slow to realize that my numerous shops, could they but get their wares into them, offered perhaps the best centres in the country for the retail distribution of tea. Here was an organization all cut and dry, with many thousands of customers, ready-made and only requiring the simplest of exploitations! That was what the wholesalers thought, and what they told me, not once but many times.

I began to toy with the idea. It seemed good to me. The arguments of the wholesalers were perfectly sound. The addition of tea to my list of comestibles for sale meant no great alteration or revision of my business arrangements. By and by, I went further into the suggestion. I discovered from the middlemen just what profits they operated upon so far as the retailers were concerned and it was obvious to me that these profits were, to say the least of it, substantial. Next I made it my duty to find out exactly what the middlemen themselves paid for their tea at Mincing Lane, London, and here again I was astonished at the difference between what they paid for the tea in the first instance and the price they were prepared to quote me, even for very large parcels. And it did not take me long to come to a two-fold decision. Namely, to enter the tea-trade with all the enthusiasm I had devoted to my other activities and to become my own wholesaler. In other words, to do what I had done in the ham, butter and egg business and cut out the middleman, with profit alike to myself and my customers.

So far, so good. I started to watch Mincing Lane and all that took place in that most famous of the world's street markets. I bought tea in small quantities to begin with. Making every allowance for overheads, I found that I could sell a first-class tea to my customers for one shilling and sevenpence per pound as against the two shillings and sixpence they were being charged for practically the same quality by the ordinary retailers. The difficulty was the blending. Experts warned me that as a new-comer I would have insuperable difficulty in prevailing upon competent tea-blenders to enter my employ; without them I could not, by any conceivable means, produce a tea which people would drink!

"Why not let well alone?" urged a Mincing Lane broker who afterwards became one of my best friends. "You don't know one-tenth of the difficulties and dangers of the tea-trade. If such a scheme as yours was as easy as you think it is, many people would have made fortunes at it before now! Tea's a difficult game for a novice to tackle, believe me!"

I assured him that tea was a perfectly intriguing proposition so far as I was concerned, and that in a year or two I hoped to be among the world's largest tea-merchants! He walked off with that look on his face which plainly says—another good man gone wrong!

Going "my ain gait", I enlisted the services of one or two men who had big reputations as expert tea-judges in London, and, with their assistance, I set out to solve the problem of blending without having recourse to the professional blenders, or offering any of them positions on my staff. In the meantime I "laid low and said nuffin' ". But I was certainly far from idle!

An epoch-making day in the history of the firm of Lipton came when, in the dining-room at Lancefield Street, I sat down with my departmental chiefs and proceeded to test the special blend of tea prepared by my London friends after many, many experiments and many, many failures. We sipped it, we drank it, we smelt it, we rolled it on our palates and on our lips, looking at each other the while. We also compared it with "brews" made from much more expensive samples. The Lipton one-and-sevenpenny tea more than held its own. In fact, we all decided that it was a tea fit for any table in the land, with a richness and a flavour which few of the other blends could equal! We called in several members of the ordinary staff and they also agreed that they had never tasted so good a "cup of tea".

So, the new tea department of Lipton's was in lively being in the course of a week or two. I believe I am merely stating a fact when I say that my entry into the British tea market created a sensation of the first magnitude. The public rushed for my tea at one-and-sevenpence a pound. They liked it so well that before many weeks had elapsed I added two other blends at a shilling and fifteenpence per pound respectively—tea-prices unheard of in the world up till that time. My branch shops were besieged morning, noon and night. The customers who came for tea alone remained to buy my other goods and the Lipton stores in every part of the country broke their trading records over and over again. In tea alone a branch which didn't sell a ton at least every week was held at headquarters to be securing poor results!

If I had been leading quite a strenuous commercial existence before setting out to grapple with this tea problem, you may well imagine that now I was just about the most preoccupied merchant in broad Scotland. Still, the joy of the business-game meant everything to me, and the bigger the task the better it pleased me. Difficulties only cropped up to be surmounted and decisions involving sums of money had to be taken at the gallop, so to speak. How I revelled in it all! Fortunately, I was able to put out of my mind, temporarily at least, all other ordinary business worries so that I could concentrate on tea and the selling of it in vast quantities under the best and simplest marketing conditions.

CHAPTER XIV

Tea in packets proves a novel success—Lipton shops abroad—comedy at the Customs with a barrel of water —a trip to Colombo for coffee—estates in Ceylon— opposition in the London markets.

ONE of the first innovations I carried into effect was to have my tea made up beforehand in pound, half-pound and quarter-pound packets. Hitherto, the general practice in the retail trade had been to serve tea from open chests or drawers behind the counter and this method, in my view, was unsatisfactory for many reasons. Chiefly because it led to uncertainty in the customer's mind as to whether she was being given the correct weight or the exact quality of tea for which she was paying. The Lipton "packets", plainly marked as to price and quality, instantly became popular. They were also much more easy to handle from the standpoint of shopkeeper and client alike.

An early discovery which I made concerning tea was that it varied in taste and "body" according to the water in which it was brewed. Thus, a blend which excellently suited one town became flat and insipid as a beverage when brewed in another town perhaps forty miles away. The explanation, of course, lies in the varying chemical properties of the different water supplies. Accordingly I issued instructions to each of my branch managers to forward, periodically, samples of the water drunk by the inhabitants of his town or city to my tea-tasters in London, and the latter, in their turn, were instructed to prepare the most suitable blends for the different districts. The result was that I was able to advertise "the perfect tea to suit the water of your own town", an idea that had never been hit upon before and which scored heavily for Lipton's teas. I know that this may sound rather far-fetched but it is nevertheless true. The tea I was selling in Edinburgh was quite a different blend from that retailed in Glasgow, while the London tea, specially blended to suit the water, was a different article altogether to the hard-water tea sent from my headquarters to Manchester, for instance.

Even when I had started my continental branches the practice of testing the water was still adhered to. I remember a shop manager returning from Hamburg with a fairly large cask of water and finding great difficulty in getting his "luggage" past the Customs. The first official who fell foul of him simply stared when he was told that the cask contained nothing but water. Then he went and called the Chief Examiner.

"Come along, now, what have you got in that cask?" demanded the chief with some asperity.

"Drinking water!" explained my manager.

It was now the chief's turn to stare. This was a

new experience in a long life spent in the customs service!

"Plain drinking water?" he demanded, nonplussed. "Do you mean to tell us that you have travelled from Hamburg with a cask of water? What do you think we are—children? Open the cask an' let's taste this precious water of yours!"

Water, of course, it was, but only after every officer at Dover had carefully tasted and sniffed it did they allow our man to pass. And from the glances they bestowed upon his retreating figure they plainly took him for a harmless lunatic!

Being now so closely in touch with Mincing Lane, I found that I had to be frequently in London, and I caused a stir in the dove-cots of the Lane by paying cash on the nail for everything I purchased, no matter how large the quantity. Being only human the brokers rather liked this, to them, new way of settling accounts. I, on my side, gained the cash discount—a not inconsiderable advantage on *my* accounts. It was around this same period that I began to look out for more branch shops in London. Already I had two—one near Whiteley's in Bayswater and the second near the Angel, at Islington.

Apropos the Islington premises I cannot resist recalling an amusing story which, even to this day, always makes me laugh when I remember it. In these days I had a manager in my employment of the name of Love. He had been in London at the

SIR THOMAS ALWAYS WORE A BLUE-SPOTTED TIE

taking-over of the Islington shop and, desiring to get in touch with the contractor who was going to make the necessary structural alterations, he wired him to his home as follows: "Meet me at the Angel at eight to-night, Love".

Mr. Love waited fully an hour for the contractor but he did not show face and my manager had to return the same night to Glasgow. A few days later he was again in London, and this time he called upon the contractor at his place of business and upbraided him for his carelessness in not keeping the appointment made by telegram.

"What telegram? I never got a telegram from you, Mr. Love!" exclaimed the man. Then suddenly a light seemed to dawn upon him. "By heavens!" he ejaculated. "I see it all now. My wife has been impossible to live with for three days. She must have opened your telegram signed Love for she certainly left the house that night and was away for two hours and came back in a devil of a temper. I must run home and explain!" And off the contractor went.

The poor man's surmise proved correct. His wife had opened the telegram. Even yet she would not accept his explanations.

"I don't believe this story about a Mr. Love—as if anybody could believe a cock-and-bull tale like that!" raved the still angry woman. "Why, I went down to the Angel and saw the woman waiting there with my own eyes. There were several other females standing round the doors but I knew her at a glance and I had hard work to keep my hands off the huzzy. You and your 'Mr. Love'!"

Not until Mr. Love had been prevailed upon by the distracted contractor to go along with him and explain matters to his wife was peace restored in that troubled household.

I had been in the tea-trade barely a year when an opportunity presented itself for me to go out to Ceylon. This was after the Coffee Crop failure in the Island. Certain London bankers, representing a group of Ceylon estates, had approached me with the object of prevailing upon me to purchase these and go in for tea-planting on a large scale. I was already buying tea in stupendous quantities; why not grow a lot of the commodity myself?—they urged. The idea did not displease me in the least. It coincided entirely with the rule I had laid down for the abolishing, wherever possible, the middleman or intermediary profiteer between the producer and the consumer. But I did not intend to buy a "pig in a poke". So instead of coming to a decision with the bankers I secretly booked a passage to Australia on the first available liner, but got off at Colombo, Ceylon.

On arriving at Colombo I at once went up-country to the Kandy and Matele tea districts where I inspected the estates for sale. Although I knew as much about tea-planting as Euclid knew about motoring I liked the look of the estates. They seemed good to me. Without further consideration of the matter I cabled off a very low offer to the London bankers and when they replied "Can't you do better?" I knew the plantations were mine! Within a few hours, and at the small additional cost of one or two more cables, I became their sole proprietor. That I was not likely to repent of my hurried bargain was made fairly clear to me no later than next morning when another would-be buyer, one with some experience, too, of the planting business came along and offered me ten thousand pounds profit on my deal.

The first estates I acquired in Ceylon were known as the Downall group in Haputale and they included the plantations known as Dambatenne, Laymostotte and Monerakande. They extended to between two and three thousand acres, but only about half the territory was "under tea and coffee". The first thing I did was to arrange that all the land should be cultivated—what was the use of spending money on waste land in Ceylon? Having embarked now as a real tea-planter I rather enjoyed the sensation, so much so that a few days later I bought another estate, this one the Pooprassie plantation at Pussellawa. Before leaving the island I made arrangements for the taking over of other properties as and when they could be secured. Between the estates I had bought and the big sum of money I left with my agent for immediate future use I think I must have invested well over a hundred thousand pounds in Ceylon within a week or two of my arrival in that lovely and delectable island of spicy breezes.

I would not like you to imagine that in these early Ceylon transactions, and in the subsequent important developments of my eastern interests, everything "came off" for me as easily as if I had been shelling peas. Far from it. A lot of hard thinking had to be done and much more hard work. Many problems had to be faced, human and economic. I had to apply myself diligently to a completely new set of facts and circumstances. "East is East and West is West!" and I speedily found it out. But, East or West, commonsense generally comes out on top and my chief aim, after becoming a tea-planter on a large scale, was to improve my properties and the conditions of my native employees, banish waste, introduce up-to-date methods and instal modern machinery. Without doing all these things I could see that my investments were not going to be so profitable as at first seemed likely.

From the beginning—or, at all events, as soon as I could get the necessary machinery—all the tea on my plantations was handled and packed, after the picking, mechanically, thus securing perfect cleanliness and greater uniformity of treatment than was possible in the system obtaining in China and Japan. Again, most of the Ceylon tea was picked far up on the hillsides and manufactured in the factories miles below in the valleys, being transported there by native carriers whose job of bearing sacks full of leaves down narrow, tortuous and dangerous mountain-paths was not one to be envied. I improved upon that method of transport by fitting up a system of what might be described as aerial "wire-ways" between my tea-gardens on the hills and the factories at their base. The tea, when gathered, was placed in strong bags fitted at the top with rings and these bags were sent whizzing down the wires right to the door of the factories. The natives themselves were delighted to see such a simple and effective contrivance take the place of their laborious journeyings up and down the mountains. In numerous other ways I reorganized the production of tea on my Ceylon estates.

"Direct from the Tea Garden to the Teapot!" This was the slogan I came home with from my trip to Ceylon and I made the utmost of it in all my advertising for several years thereafter. It must have made a very strong appeal, too, for my sales of tea went up by leaps and bounds. Often, in spite of my Ceylon supplies and the great parcels I continued to purchase in Mincing Lane and latterly at the Colombo Tea Sales I was actually hard put to it to let all my branches have all that they required so that my millions of customers could be satisfied. Statements of quantities passing through my hands at this time would convey very little to the mind of the ordinary man or woman,

but I may say that within a few months of my
entering the trade I paid in one cheque to the
Customs Authorities of Great Britain a sum of
£15,000 odd as duty on tea cleared from bond.
Later I paid many cheques of from twenty to thirty
thousand pounds and I finally eclipsed all customs
records for Britain by signing a cheque for the
tremendous sum of £50,513 11s. 6d., this representing a customs clearance of nearly three million
pounds of tea. Even this big figure was beaten in
still later years.

Naturally the newspapers could not refrain from
publishing such tit-bits—and I took no step to
prevent them doing so! They also wrote up many
glowing accounts of my Ceylon activities. Only
the other day I was glancing over my cuttings books
—which, let me say, occupy an entire bookcase in
one of the rooms of my house in London—and I
came across this paragraph, cut from one of the
leading London newspapers: "Mr. Lipton's recent
purchase of tea estates in Ceylon marks the opening of a new era in British trading. Never before
has the owner of tea estates undertaken to act as
his own retailer. From this daring and unique
method of trading between the planter and the
public the masses must inevitably stand to profit."
And profit they certainly did. I continued to sell
my blends of tea at prices which other dealers could
not hope to contend with. Some of them tried
their best to discredit me in the eyes of the public

by spreading abroad the rumour that only by selling an inferior article was I in a position to charge such ridiculous prices. Indeed, it was hinted in various quarters that I was losing vast sums of money in the tea business and that I was only "keeping on" to save my face.

In Mincing Lane opposition against me became rife. It was but to be expected that the man who was running his own plantations and selling "direct from the tea garden to the teapot" would not be joyfully received in the Lane devoted to brokers and middlemen, but all the same I got as much tea as I wanted there because they knew that my money was good and always forthcoming on the spot. Several attempts were made to belittle "cheap tea" by running up prices for specially-selected and extra fine packets of tea to as much as five and ten guineas per pound. However, I proved more than a match for tactics of this kind. To prove to the Lane and to the public that my estates in Ceylon were capable of producing the best tea in the universe I cabled my manager in the island to send me home a parcel of the very finest, gold-tipped tea grown on our own ground. In due course it arrived and was sold by public auction in Mincing Lane at the amazing price of thirty-six guineas per pound! After this there was no further attempt to decry Lipton's tea; it had set up a record difficult, almost impossible, to beat.

Latterly, I started to draw largely on India as

well as Ceylon for my supplies. Incidentally, I set up prosperous retail organizations both at Calcutta and Colombo. The fact that I, a Glasgow Irishman, had had the audacity to start selling tea to the people of the countries in which it was grown rather appealed to my sense of humour.

CHAPTER XV

South Omaha as a pork-packing centre—my employees carry firearms—a deal with Mr. P. D. Armour—I decide to popularize tea-drinking in America—a huge success.

SOON, the large supplies of "Lipton" tea I had available in India and Ceylon led me to the decision to break direct into the American tea-trade. Supplies for my home market no longer gave me any uneasiness for I had purchased several more plantations, so that I had ample margins of supplies for prospective American customers provided I could prevail upon them to become addicted to my tea in the same way as I had come to be a firm believer in their hams and bacons and cheese.

My relationship with the American people has been so close and cordial for such a number of years that I hardly need say that, when I resolved to become a tea merchant in the United States I made one of the happiest decisions in my life. But even before I took this momentous step, I had closely cemented my associations with the Americans both as regards personal friendships and business relations. From the year 1883, when I had set up my first pork-packing house in

Chicago, right up till 1890 I had been paying very frequent visits to the other side of the Atlantic. I had conceived an admiration and an affection for the people over there which made it difficult for me to stay long away from their hospitable shores. I always say that if anybody should know America and the American people it is myself, for I have travelled amongst them like a prince and I have travelled amongst them stone-broke. The only fault I have to find with them is that they nail down my trunks so that I can't get away from them!

The Cork Packing Company in Chicago had only been in existence three years when it was obvious to me that it had outgrown its clothes. Even working day and night it could not cope with the demands of my business at home. In Chicago one day I was looking around for a new location for a larger factory when, over the luncheon table at my hotel, I heard that good land was going a-begging at South Omaha, Nebraska, simply for want of a pork-packer with enterprise enough to develop it. I put sufficient faith into the source of the information to take train next day for this, at that period, practically unexplored region. To-day, South Omaha is one of the most thriving centres of the pork-packing industry, but away back in the 'eighties it was a very small place indeed and had a poorly-developed railroad service. To tell the truth I wasn't over-impressed with the possibilities of South Omaha after my experience of

SHAMROCK IV—THE BEST OF ALL THE *SHAMROCKS*:
AMERICA'S CUP CHALLENGER, 1914-1920

Chicago, and my first inclination was to take the earliest train back to the latter city.

But, as it happened, two men with whom I got into touch before I could carry out my half-formed resolve, prevailed upon me to sit down and discuss the situation. They were Mr. Paxton, of the Paxton Hotel, and Mr. Gallacher, a local merchant. Between them they owned a strip of land on the outskirts of Omaha, and they did their best to convince me that this land was ideal for the establishment of such a factory as I had in view. They went further than this—they actually offered to build me a large packing-house *free of all charge whatever* if I would agree to start operations in their town and on their land! Confronted with such a magnificent and sporting offer, I agreed to accept it on the spot. An agreement was drawn up between us forthwith, the sole "condition" laid down by my friends, Messrs. Paxton and Gallacher, being that I should "kill" every day for a specified number of years. But we all forgot to specify the number of hogs to be killed per day. Legally, the killing and dressing of one hog each day would have implemented my contract!

My new factory was duly built and put in operation, and I am proud to think that I was one of the pioneers in building up the town of South Omaha. In the work of developing my new packing-house we had somewhat unusual conditions to face. An American town in the making inevitably attracts all sorts and conditions of men, and in a district so "woolly" and uncultivated as Omaha was at that time this was especially the case. The first time I visited the "Lipton Packing Company's" building after it had been built and was in full running order, I was quite surprised to learn that the watchmen and certain other of the employees carried firearms. Frequently tramps and rough customers would look in during the day and inquire blandly if there "was a job going". Often there was, but when there wasn't it was no unusual thing for these gentry to pull out their guns and, in effect, proceed on the principle "A job or your life!" I have never forgotten the first peep I took into the cloak-room of my place at South Omaha. Pistols were lying about all over the place and protruded from many of the coats and jackets hanging on the hooks. It reminded me of an armoury!

The task of managing hundreds of men who had such a downright way of looking after themselves would have been no light task but for the fact that I insisted upon the best and most friendly relationships existing between the proprietor and his workers. There was never the shadow of friction. The new packing-house prospered exceedingly. Not only was it capable of supplying most of my British requirements, but the output was so large that I began to deal with buyers in different parts of the American continent. Of many contracts I secured one was for 500 tons of smoked bacon from

the Alaska Commercial Company, whose headquarters were in San Francisco, and one of the
conditions laid down was that it had to be packed
in certain sized crates with rope handles attached
suitable for Klondyke miners carrying with them on
prospecting tours. A special Lipton train conveyed
this vast quantity of bacon to the Pacific coast,
where it was transferred to a waiting steamer and
therein carried to the nearest port to Dawson City.
This was a good advertisement for me and, combined with other spectacular deals, it caused my
American trade to swell with every succeeding
month. At South Omaha I was four hundred miles
nearer the west coast centres than was Chicago and,
my freight charges being correspondingly less, I was
enabled to sell stuff all over the west at prices which
the Chicago packers found difficult to compete
against.

The requirements of the growing American
section of my trade being rather different from those
of my English customers, I latterly split up my
Omaha output into two brands, one being sold under
the name of the Lipton Packing Company and the
other under the name of the Johnstone Packing
House—the "Johnstone" being taken, I may
explain, from my own middle name. And it says
something for the quality of my American "brand"
of produce that at one time I had a contract from
the powerful firm of "Armours" for the supply of
a thousand dressed hogs per day! Indeed, Mr.

Michael Cudahy, who was then the partner of
Mr. P. D. Armour, came to me himself on one of
my visits to the middle west and suggested that I
might perhaps be willing to part with my interests
in the new factory to the Armour people. At first
I showed no disposition to sell, but I formed a very
high opinion of Mr. Cudahy, as honest and upright
a man as ever lived and with whom I was on terms
of goodwill ever afterwards. A few months later,
however, I met his partner, Mr. Armour, and he, on
his part, renewed the offer on such a handsome and
generous scale that I decided to accept it. Frankly,
my Omaha packing-house had one disadvantage.
English people have a decided liking for a leaner
variety of bacon and ham than that most suited to
American tastes, and the hogs reared on the rich
grain lands of Nebraska were just a trifle too fat for
the British trade. So, taking one consideration with
another, I made a very sound "deal" when I sold
out to Mr. Armour.

Always, I found the great "P. D." a splendid
man—open, frank, and generously kind in all his
transactions. He had a warm-hearted smile and
fine, strong hand-shake, the same sort of put-it-
there grip which characterized the late President
Roosevelt. We completed the bargain on Independence Day.

After the sale of my packing-house at South
Omaha I was compelled to return to Chicago, and
here I temporarily leased premises to tide me over

against the day when I could establish another factory big enough for my necessities. The opportunity came along in a few weeks when I found that an extensive building named the Meyer Packing House was for sale. On making a personal inspection of it, I made up my mind that here was the very building I required. There was only one difficulty. If it became known that I was after the property, certain of my competitors would be dead sure to chip in with bids and thus run up the price against me. Naturally I didn't want to pay more than I could get off with; and naturally, as I was not too conversant personally with what would be a reasonable price to pay, I had to rely on my trusted friend, Mr. John Craig Hateley, who always acted for me as my adviser in all my Chicago deals. On this occasion Mr. Hateley's methods as go-between at the conference when the sale was effected were certainly original. Since I knew so little of what would be an adequate price to pay, how could I appear at this important business interview without giving my ignorance away? Such was our problem. But Mr. Hateley solved it. Each time a price was mentioned by the vendors which he considered too high, he blew his nose vigorously, and this was a sign to me to protest with equal vigour and offer a much smaller figure. The vendors were considerably surprised at such amazing knowledge of actual values, and when at length Mr. Hateley ceased to show signs of a cold in the head, I knew the offer was reasonable and closed the deal.

I heard later that I had secured the property at the rock-bottom price at which they were prepared to sell.

Mr. Hateley thoroughly enjoyed this incident. Often in later years we laughed over it together. John Craig Hateley was a staunch friend, a shrewd man of business—keen, always a worker, and always on the level.

My purchase of the Meyer house proved to be a sound investment. It covered four and a half acres of ground and very soon I was killing 2,000 to 4,000 hogs per day. I established a fleet of express refrigerator cars with the one word "Lipton" painted on them from end to end, and these cars travelled all over the American continent carrying my products and advertising them wherever they went.

I must now revert back to the story of my breaking into the American tea market. If I have wandered from it, I have done so with one object, namely, to show by this time I was no stranger in the United States. Indeed, I was spending fully as much time there as in my own land. New York was as familiar to me as Glasgow, and Chicago was a sort of third home. I had formed close personal and business friendships—friendships which were to last many, many years and to be broken only, in too numerous instances, by the visitations of the Grim Reaper. Glad I am to think, however, that

I still have countless business and sporting ties with
America.

Whenever I discovered that I was going to be
in a position to handle more tea than I required
for my British and ordinary export trades, my
thoughts naturally crossed the Atlantic Ocean.
What about introducing my tea to the great new
public over there? I asked myself. Here was a field
worthy of attack, a practically limitless market for
an enterprising merchant confident of the quality
of his wares. The habit, or custom, of tea-drinking
was increasing rapidly in Britain—the weekly
returns from my branch shops confirmed that fact
beyond doubt or question—and I saw no reason
why the habit should not soon be spreading to the
United States. Pondering over these problems
during a westward Atlantic passage, I decided to
give the American tea-trade the "once-over" on my
arrival. A day or two spent in investigations here
and there might well prove profitable, I told myself.
In any case no harm could be done.

Almost at the very outset of these investigations
I was astonished beyond measure. To all intents
and purposes there was *no* tea-trade in America. I
started by asking for a cup of tea in my hotel the
first morning I was ashore, and the waiter looked
at me with an expression of blank amazement. It
was almost as if he had never heard of tea in his
life! He went off scratching his head and repeating
the words: "Tea, sir? Did you say tea, sir?" At

the finish he brought me coffee and added that "the stuff I asked for was not stocked in this hotel". I found the same state of affairs in other hotels and in restaurants. Tea of a kind was certainly obtainable in some of the stores, both in New York and in Chicago, and I bought samples just to see what manner of drink these produced when "masked", as we would say in Scotland. Without exception they were terrible—at least, to my taste. For the most part the teas sold to the general public were "Oolongs" and "Japans", common sorts of green teas, and a most inferior "China Congou". Many of the store-keepers regarded tea as on the same level with barley, rice, and maize, and kept their supplies exposed in all kinds of open receptacles. At a leading grocery establishment on State Street, Chicago, I saw tea being made to suffer the horrible indignity of complete exposure to all kinds of weather at the open shop door. And even for the poor qualities of tea on offer excessive charges were made. Several times I went into stores and asked for a pound of Ceylon tea. Always the reply was that tea "from that place" was unknown in America. In addition to all this the tea, when it *was* asked for, was supplied in cheap paper-bags, minus all that dainty attractiveness in wrapping, and almost reverent handling, to which good tea is entitled!

I decided to tackle the proposition at once. To begin with I had a notion to set up in the retail provision trade in America in much the same way

SIR THOMAS WITH TOM MIX AND JACK DEMPSEY

as I had done in my own country. This idea pleased me for a time and I was supported in it by many friends in New York and Chicago. Others, again, thought I would be well-advised, for various considerations, to confine myself to the wholesale side so far as America was concerned. After weighing up all the pros and cons, I came to the conclusion that the latter course was the wiser to pursue.

As a preliminary canter, and primarily with the object of testing out the situation so far as selling Lipton's teas were concerned, I appointed a large number of agents who set to work on the best methods of getting my tea into hotels, restaurants, and private houses. I selected my men with discrimination, and I suppose I must have imbued them with some of my own enthusiasm, because in less than no time thousands of orders came rolling in to my Chicago headquarters. Luckily I had had the foresight to forward fairly large supplies from Ceylon, but within a few weeks I had to employ the cables both to London and my Ceylon headquarters for the urgent ordering of further supplies. My good friend, Mr. P. D. Armour, was one of my first private customers, and I still treasure a letter he sent me soon after my adventuring into the tea business in the States. It read as follows:

> I consider both my own house and the homes of my relatives are incomplete unless they are well supplied with Lipton's Teas. We cannot get tea anywhere in our country to give us anything like the same satisfaction.

This was a magnificent advertisement for me and, needless to say, I made the best possible use of it!

Great retailers and many other merchants controlling popular stores all over the States willingly agreed to take large parcels of tea from me, and their customers, in turn, being delighted with the new and cheap beverage associated with my name, I found myself firmly established in the American tea market. Actually, within eighteen months of my initial visit to Ceylon and buying my first plantations, I was selling more tea in America and Canada than ever I had hoped to do. Yet I was not at all satisfied with my rate of progress. So I sat down and worked out a scheme of advertising covering the whole of the American continent from New York to San Francisco and from Toronto to New Orleans. I forget just how much money I spent in this, my first American advertising campaign, but it must have run to hundreds of thousands of dollars. Did it justify itself?—you ask. It did—thoroughly. That was forty years ago this year, and I am proud to think that "Thomas J. Lipton, Incorporated", whose headquarters are at Hoboken and whose large sky-sign is a familiar landmark to New Yorkers and to every transatlantic traveller, is as flourishing to-day as ever it was in its long history.

This is a very brief account of the founding of the Lipton tea business in America. I could easily have elaborated it to much greater length and told many interesting and amusing incidents which cropped up in the course of my efforts to convert the people of the United States and Canada into a tea-drinking community. But I feel that I must now hurry on to other important events in my life.

CHAPTER XVI

MEANWHILE, I was fortunate inasmuch as the barometer of my commercial prosperity at home continued to rise even while I was devoting so much time and attention to the United States and Canadian ends of my organization. On my return from New York in the autumn of 1890, I experienced a curious dual sensation of elation and misgiving. I could not, on the one hand, but be overjoyed to find great strides still being made by the business all over Britain; but my satisfaction on this score was sadly tempered by the gradually failing health of my father and mother. They were both now over eighty years of age. I had set up a comfortable home for them and for myself at Cambuslang. They had everything they wanted, even down to the "carriage-and-pair" for my mother, which, as a wee boy, I had confidently promised she would ride in "some day". My mother enjoyed thoroughly the sensation of driving behind two spanking horses, but I think she enjoyed even more the little pleasantry which always obtained between us when, as sometimes happened, I wanted to please her by humbly asking if I could have the use of the carriage for an hour or two.

"Mother," I would say of a morning, "will you lend me your carriage, so that I can drive to the office?"

"Only on one condition, Tom," she would reply, her face lighting up with a smile. "That is that you keep the carriage to drive you all day long and bring you home in the evening!"

Looking back on these days, I recall how only two years ago, while staying at my hotel in New York, an old gentleman called to see me and told me that he knew my parents and myself in Scotland, and he reminded me of an incident which I had entirely forgotten. It seemed that one morning I had a little "tiff" with my mother just as I was about to set out for my day's work; so we did not part on our usual affectionate terms. But during my six miles' drive to my office, I felt very unhappy about this and found it quite impossible to start work.

At first I thought of telegraphing to make my peace, but then decided that I must go right back home and put matters right with both of us.

When I arrived at the house, I pretended at first to be in as much of a tantrum as ever. But it was no use. My mother was not to be deceived, and said: "I know well enough what you've come back for, Tom," and there was no more to be said. I went back to my work at peace with myself and everybody else because I had left my mother happy.

When she died on February 1st, 1889, I lost my best friend and trustiest counsellor. Without her unfaltering love, her constant encouragements, her amazing shrewdness and foresight, I could never have fought the business battles I did or achieved one tithe of the success that came my way. A few months later my father slipped quietly away to join the wife he loved, leaving me a sad and very lonely man. I am lonely to-day, for I have not one living relative in the world.

Soon after the death of my parents I had to face a pretty serious problem. The constant growth of my tea business, both at home and abroad, called still more and more for my attendance in London. Moreover, my shops in England had multiplied so largely that my interests "across the border" were imperatively demanding a headquarters organization much nearer than Glasgow. In other words, London was gradually becoming the real hub of the Lipton outfit. I found myself spending half my life in railway trains between Glasgow and the metropolis and vice versa, while my principal colleagues were doing the same thing. For the money which the firm was spending in railway fares it could have hired a series of Lipton Special Trains, with constant steam up on the engines!

But for sentimental reasons I delayed taking the obvious step for several months. Glasgow was my birthplace. I had started my career as a merchant there. To uproot my office and factory organization would be a task of great magnitude. Hundreds of people would have to be transplanted to a new soil and, to a great extent, new conditions. I pondered over these problems for quite a long time. At last I made up my mind. London was the place. Taking up the telephone in my private room at Lancefield Street, I got through on the trunk line to my London manager. I had a suite of offices, a small factory, and a considerable strip of ground in Bath Street, City Road, practically in the heart of London, but I was not sure myself whether sufficiently large premises could be erected here to house my entire headquarters' staff. So I set myself to find out. When I got the call through, I said to my London manager:

"How long will it take you to make the necessary arrangements for accommodating the whole of Lancefield Street in London—and do you think it can be done at Bath Street?"

The London manager paused for a few moments and then promptly replied: "Six weeks! And we can do it in Bath Street!"

"Very good," I remarked. "We all start in London at nine o'clock in the morning six weeks from to-day."

And we did—almost to the minute arranged.

The coming of the Lipton army to London was of the nature of a small invasion. Scots are constantly arriving in London—just as they are always stepping off the gang-planks at New York—but it is seldom that a thousand of them arrive together *en masse*, as the Lipton "clan" did. However, they all settled down very quickly and happily in London, proving once again the astonishing adaptability of their race. Give a Scot plenty of work, good wages, and a glance at an occasional Glasgow newspaper and he'll be happy and contented in Hankow or Timbuctoo or Spitzbergen! And happiest of all in London! They'll tell you that the "competition" there isn't so keen as in their own land.

Writing about this sudden transference of my headquarters staff to England reminds me of an amusing talk I had one morning with my mother's old coachman. This worthy man had insisted on coming with me to London as one of my personal servants, and he was a member of my household when I established myself in a nice but unpretentious villa in Muswell Hill, London, and the ways of Londoners interested him tremendously. At first he seldom went far from the vicinity of the pleasant suburb in which my villa was situated, but one day he seemed to have wandered into the confines of the city itself and to have been vastly impressed with, among other things, the London business men's custom of wearing glossy silk hats. When I got home in the evening, he asked me if I would mind telling him "what great man was dead?"

Puzzled at the strange question, I replied that I could not. "How do you know that a great man is dead?" I asked him.

"Oh, sir," he replied, "there's been the biggest funeral in London to-day ye ever saw in yer life. The 'departed' must have been a Royal personage, or a Prime Minister, or a General, or somebody verra famous!"

"That's strange," I remarked. "I heard nothing about it, and there's certainly nothing in the papers to-night about any great man dying. Are you sure?"

"Oh, quite sure, sir," persisted the good fellow, "because I saw thoosands an' thoosands o' men and ilka ane o' them was wearin' a lum-hat an' black claes!"

To show what the departure of Lipton's from Glasgow meant to trade of that city I might mention that it was calculated my "flitting" to London caused an immediate loss to the Scottish postal authorities of nearly a thousand pounds a week in stamps and telegraphic and cable fees. I did not work out the amount myself, but it was figured up by a Glasgow journalist. Apropos—the local newspapers regretted my going, but wished me and the firm every success in England. One of them published an amusing "obituary" notice as follows:

> Mr. Thomas Lipton has lived among us so long as one of the Commissariat Department of our community that Glasgow without him will not be the same place at all.

He piles the mountainous cheeses, Alps upon Alps, and girdles the globe with his sausages. He brings his tea from the Orient and collects his spices from Araby with as much certainty as if they grew in a back-garden in Sauchiehall Street. His ambassadors are everywhere, so that doom is writ on the ox of the American plains or the pig that roams the bog of Connemara. When Lipton invades a town every citizen knows it. His name is in their mouths. He adds shop to shop and story to story, and his servants swell to the proportions of an army for the routing of the Giant Hunger. And now, alas! the great Lipton is evacuating our city!

But while this tribute was obviously too flattering, not to say fulsome, the citizens of Glasgow were not slow to realize that at least a very progressive business had been established amongst them. It meant employment to several thousands and, even more to the point, cheap and good food for the masses. As an example of the up-to-date manner in which we worked, I may recall here that we were one of the first business houses in Britain to instal typewriting machines. Which reminds me of the day when an English traveller called at my head-quarters and happened to see two girls clicking away at their typewriters. Turning to me with a mystified air, he remarked:

"I know, Mr. Lipton, that you are in the butter, cheese, ham, and egg trade, but it's news to me that you have started to make shirts!" He actually thought the typewriters were sewing-machines.

The years immediately succeeding the arrival of Lipton's in London probably marked the greatest

SHAMROCK V APPEARING TO BE IN THE LEAD JUST AFTER
THE START OF THE FIRST RACE, WHICH *ENTERPRISE*
ULTIMATELY WON VERY EASILY

advance in the history of the firm. Still feeling very much the deaths of my mother and father and a sense of utter loneliness taking possession of me, I threw myself more strenuously than ever into the maelstrom of business. Headquarters were enlarged again and again, until they occupied many acres at City Road. New shops were acquired in every likely corner of the kingdom. Metropolitan and provincial factories were set up. Jam was added to the commodities I sold, and fruit farms had to be purchased to make certain of adequate supplies. From proprietor to office-boy we worked early and late. Orders were always ahead of fulfilment. New business was constantly coming along and new methods being tried out. One of the heads of the many building firms employed by me about this time tersely described the situation so far as Lipton's was concerned when he turned to me rather sharply one morning and remarked:

"The trouble with your firm is that it is like a boy who grows so fast that he needs a new suit of clothes every week!"

I continued to be one of the largest advertisers in England, using the columns of every paper of any standing, both daily and weekly. At all the big "fairs" and "expositions" (as they were sometimes called) I was a competitor. From the Chicago Exhibition of 1893 I brought away the highest awards for tea, coffee, and coffee essence; actually I won so many prizes at functions like this all over the world that I got tired of entering!

It honestly seemed to me that about this time in my business career everything conspired to keep my name always before the public. If a fire occurred which destroyed a large section of my headquarter premises in London, it received far more attention from the newspapers than the event really merited because, as it so happened, there was left standing, grim, gaunt, and prominent, an immense signboard built of iron and bearing the name of the firm—triumphant, the papers pointed out, over the devouring element!

For many years after establishing my organization in London I lived, as the phrase has it, for nothing else but my work. It was my joy to be continually immersed in the big developments of the business and to take a fatherly interest in the great human machine which had grown up around me. Each day was the same—at my desk early in the morning and home late to bed. I had few personal friends apart from my enormous family of employees—ten thousand of them and scattered throughout the world in plantations, factories, stores, and warehouses. With these I tried to keep in close touch always. If I ever entertained at home, it was to the simplest of dinners, and the party was generally confined to three or four only. I seldom went to the theatre or attended any public function. My one luxury—apart from an occasional holiday, which I compelled myself to take and which provided me with the necessary change of scene and reinvigorated mental outlook—was the possession of a team of fast Kentucky trotting horses behind which, the reins in my own hands, I generally drove to and from the office.   Later I became one of the first British motor enthusiasts— but that is another story!

While all that I have written about my engrossing interest in the affairs of my one-man firm is perfectly true, I would not like anybody to think that I believed in a life completely and wholly devoted to the sterner aspects of existence. Far from it. I certainly worked hard. But, when I did decide to take a holiday, I played just as hard. Sometimes I combined business with pleasure on my jaunts abroad; at other times I went off to the four corners of the world in the most care-free spirit. And nothing gives me greater pleasure to-day than to recall some of my experiences as a "tourist" in different lands.

CHAPTER XVII

*Reminiscences of holidays abroad—I discover I am
known in Burma—Coney Island's Devil—adventures
in Turkey—a too-faithful guide—misadventures at sea.*

ONLY the other day my friend, Colonel Duncan
Neil, and I were swapping reminiscences, and we
laughed once more over a highly-amusing adventure which befel us in Mandalay. We had been
doing a holiday trip all over the East and the opportunity occurred to visit a Buddhist temple at the
famous Burma city. When we got to the temple
we found a congress of native priests in progress.
Part of the day's ceremonials was an imposing
procession of these dignitaries and the Colonel and
I watched the picturesque and stately "march of
the Priests". Noticing that one of their number,
a very powerfully-built man with a peculiarly-
piercing eye, turned his head and stared scowlingly
in my face, I observed to my companion that I
would not like to meet the fellow alone in the dark.
The words had no sooner left my mouth than the
formidable-looking Indian priest stepped aside and
came up to me, much to my perturbation.

"Hullo, Lipton, what brings you out to this part
of the world?" he asked, speaking in a strong, Irish
accent. "I could scarcely believe my eyes when I
saw you standing amongst the crowd, but, of course,

I knew you at once from your photographs in the papers!"

I was so amazed that I almost lost the power of speech.

"Who and what are you, for goodness sake?" I asked.

"I'm Kelly, the Burmese priest!" was his reply and I thought I could detect a twinkle in his eye, even if he was tanned the colour of brown paper and wore the trappings of an Eastern holy man. "I came from Ireland originally," he went on to explain in the most affable fashion, "but I was wrecked off the coast of Burma. Liking the country, I stayed on, became converted to the Buddhist faith and was made a priest. Now I am the chief priest!" he concluded proudly.

"Well, Chief Priest Kelly," I said, having by this time got over my nervousness. "I hope you will come and see me at my hotel."

"No, no, that's a place for Christians and I cannot go there," he protested vigorously.

"But you'll be coming to see me," I reminded him.

"Oh, well, that will be different," he agreed, and sure enough, the same evening he turned up and we had a long chat together on the veranda of the hotel. Profound, indeed, was the astonishment of the other guests to see me sitting in a corner and talking volubly with the Chief Priest of Mandalay.

After "Kelly" had gone, one of the ladies came up to me and said: "How perfectly wonderful you are, sir, to be able to talk to the natives in their own language!" Anxious not to spoil the good impression I had made I explained to the lady that I did a very extensive business in the East, and, of course, if one couldn't speak the various languages it was difficult to get along.

From priest to devil ought not to be a natural step at all, but always in my mind the story of Kelly the Burmese priest is associated with another yarn which I tell, and generally I link up both stories by saying it is as well to have friends in both places—the upper and the lower regions. One evening some years ago a party of us yachting men on board a ship of mine lying off Sandy Hook found we had nothing to do and we decided to go over to Coney Island. Everybody knows, of course, that "Coney" is the greatest place in the world for side-shows. One of the attractions on the night of our visit was simply labelled "Hell".

"This may be the only chance some of us will ever have of seeing what the place is like!" one of us remarked—and so we all trooped in. I can assure my readers that I felt very far from being at home in the infernal regions, especially when the "Devil" himself cast his eye on me and his face lit up in a smile of glad recognition as if I were a long-lost brother. During the "entertainment"—or whatever it was supposed to be—he hardly ever allowed his glance to leave me and I felt relieved to be coming away when, suddenly as my party was about to leave the booth, the Coney Island Beelzebub rushed towards me and pulling me into a dark corner, he said:

"I never expected to see you here, Sir Thomas. You won't remember me, but I used to work in your Greenock shop!" Considering the influential position my old assistant now held, I thought it best to keep friendly!

Many years ago I went as far afield as Turkey for a brief holiday. Some of the incidents of that trip are still fresh in my mind. For instance, I shall never forget an experience I had with the hordes of would-be native guides who plague the lives of the foreign visitors. No sooner did I set foot in Constantinople than an entire regiment of these guides clustered round me. They looked like tearing me limb from limb. Each seemed to regard me as his special prey, gesticulating wildly, jumping in front of me and behind me, and shouting in pidgin-English. I was at my wits' end how to select one from amongst the horde, but, I reflected, if I selected one the others would probably fight for the possession of my dead body, and so I resolved to have no guide at all. I tried to explain this to the rascals and walked off on a sightseeing round.

For an hour or two a dozen or more followed my every footstep, but later in the day the number was reduced to six and nothing I could do would prevail upon this faithful band to leave me. Once I sought refuge in a carpet-shop to buy a carpet to take home to my mother, but the guides came right in after me. Trying to regard them as non-existent, I haggled with the shopkeeper over what he was going to charge me for the carpet; it was an exorbitant price, I explained to him, but he protested he could not let me have it for less because my six guides would each require a commission!

This convinced me that life in Stamboul would not be worth living unless I got rid of my body-guard of guides. So a bright idea occurred to me. Picking out the most persistent of the robbers, I told him that he could act as my guide if he got rid of all the others. Strangely enough, as soon as I had put this proposition forward and it had sunk into his head he managed magically to dismiss his rivals with a mere wave of the hand. And for the rest of that day he dogged me closely. I began most cordially to hate him and evolved a plan for getting rid of him on the morrow.

"What o'clock, O Master, shall we set forth in the morning?" he asked me as I reached the hotel steps.

"Not before half-past ten," I replied, secretly resolving to be up and about two hours earlier.

But did he believe me? No. On opening my bed-room door very early next morning, I found him sleeping on the mat and nearly tripped over him.

"Yes, it is I, Master," he leered. "And ready!" Admiring such persistence, I re-engaged him for another day's sightseeing. In business I have always encouraged the man who could prove that he was "doing his best". And sure enough this wily old Turk proved it.

I think it was during this holiday that I had a quaint experience with an elderly Greek which makes me smile every time I recall it. I had booked a state-room on a steamer making an overnight passage from one part of the Orient to another. On getting aboard, I was shown to my state-room, and, to my annoyance, I found that it was a double-berth room. In one of the bunks was lying a very stout man, obviously, by his loud snores, fast asleep. As there was no other cabin available, I had just to grin and bear the coming discomforts.

In order to brush my teeth before retiring to bed, I took up a glass half-filled with water and threw the contents out the open port-hole. My dental ablutions being performed, I got into bed and was soon in the land of Nod. I was suddenly awakened about seven o'clock by a most terrible uproar in the cabin. The old gentleman was standing in his night-dress, yelling at the pitch of his voice to a steward whom he had summoned, and doing everything that a thoroughly angry man can do to show his wrath.

From the enraged glances he was giving in my

direction, I could see that in some way I was suspect. Then the steward came over to me and explained. My fellow-passenger was on his way home from Athens where he had gone to have a new set of teeth fitted. He had the teeth last night when he came on board. He had them in the cabin when he went to sleep—not in his mouth but in a glass on the wash-stand. They were now nowhere to be found. Did I know anything of this diabolical theft? Had I seen the teeth? Had I stolen them? Did I know anything about them? The old Greek was so aflame with fury that I thought it better to sham complete ignorance of the whole matter. But, pointing to my baggage and my clothes hanging beside my bed, I indicated that any search they cared to undertake would not be resented by me. And search the two of them did —everything in the cabin was turned upside down. At last, in desperation, the Greek seized me by the jaw, forcibly opened my mouth and had a good look therein to make sure I wasn't wearing his false teeth! I afterwards learned that the entire crew were turned out to search the ship from stem to stern for the Greek's missing denture.

CHAPTER XVIII

A pencil-sketch by Lord Dewar—"The Two Scotch Toms"—Lipton's Tea in Sicily—Lord Dewar tells a story of an election campaign in which the Chancellor of the Exchequer's coat is sold—Lord Inverforth and Sir Harry Lauder—the great Scots comedian comes back to Osidge in a van.

THE late Lord Dewar—whose death over a year ago was a tremendous blow to me—was one of my best friends for forty years. Many were the trips we made together. No more amusing companion could be imagined. He was my honoured guest on many occasions at home and abroad. He went over to America with me for my Cup Challenge in 1920 and delighted the Americans with his witty speeches, full of sparkling epigrams, as well as by his quiet, charming personality. Wherever we happened to be all over the world we kept up a bantering correspondence either by letter or cable. Dewar was a very fine artist. He could have made money by his pencil and brush had he not found it easier to get by selling the brand of liquid with which his name will always be associated. He used to take keen pleasure in drawing my face on a post-card and addressing it to the country which I was visiting for the time being. Thus he would sketch me in yachting rig-out and simply put the letters "U.S.A." underneath. The American postal authorities always delivered the card without a minute's delay. Once when he was in Central Africa he sent me a cable as follows: "You can buy three wives here for six pounds of Lipton's tea. Why not come out?" I replied: "Am sending out the tea. Send samples of the wives!" Lord Dewar did not reply; nor did he send the samples!

On one occasion Dewar went into one of my shops in Harrogate, Yorkshire, and said he was an inspector from the head office. He was shown all over the premises, he examined the books, and, on leaving, said he was so satisfied with the way the shop was run that he would give everybody on the staff an increase in their salaries of one pound per week. He was easily the most popular "inspector" that had ever visited Harrogate. This joke was certainly with his lordship, for I had not the heart to stop the "increases" and went on paying them.

"The Two Scotch Toms", as we came to be called, were always trying to score off each other, but ever in the most friendly spirit. On one occasion we were visiting Taormina in Sicily, on board my yacht. With us was the late Kennedy Jones, one of Lord Northcliffe's associates in the founding of the *Daily Mail*. "K. J." wanted to get hold of a copy of his paper and said he was almost certain to find it on sale in the town.

SIR THOMAS LIPTON AT THE CITY HALL, NEW YORK, WHEN HE WAS PRESENTED WITH
A SOLID GOLD CUP FOR HIS "NEVER SAY DIE" SPIRIT

"You'll have as much chance of getting the *Daily Mail* down here as Lipton would have of getting a pound of his tea!" jocularly said Dewar. I said nothing, and we all went ashore together. Later in the day we called at the biggest store in the town and Kennedy Jones asked airily for the *Daily Mail.* The shopkeeper looked blankly at him; he had never heard of it. Then I chipped in with a request for a bottle of Dewar's whisky. Again the attendant shrugged his shoulders. Thinking then that it was up to him to complete the discomfiture of all three of us, Lord Dewar asked for a pound of Lipton's Tea. The Italian smiled broadly and intelligently. *"Si, si, Signor!"* he murmured and promptly produced the article desired! You ought to have seen the looks on the faces of my two friends as we left the shop. It was one up for "Tea Tom" that day!

Lord Dewar and I were returning from a trip to the South of France some years ago. On arrival at Calais he bought several English penny papers and handed them to me to take care of until we got on board the ship. I was one of the first aboard and happened to be standing at the top of the gangway with the papers under my arm and wearing my yachting cap when an American gentleman came up and addressed me. He evidently took me for a newspaper-seller, for he brusquely asked me if I had a *New York Herald.* Entering into the spirit of the thing I replied "No, sir, I don't think I have a *New York Herald,* but I've got the *Daily Telegraph*—I hope that will do!"

"All right, my man," said the American. "Give me the *Telegraph.* How much is it?"

Thinking to make a profit on the transaction and thus have a good story to tell Dewar I replied that the price was twopence. The stranger took the paper and disappeared. Going in search of my friend I found him in the smoke-room and gleefully reported that I had earned him some money.

"I'm always glad to hear that sort of news," said his lordship. "How did you manage to do it?"

I explained that I had been mistaken for a newsboy and just what happened.

"You are a bit of a fool," he angrily exclaimed. "Don't ye know that the price o' the *Daily Telegraph* in France is threepence and that instead of making a profit you've lost me a penny—thirty-three and a third per cent dead loss!"

Lord Dewar was a magnificent story-teller. A yarn with which he used to regale his friends had to do with the time he represented in the British Parliament a rather rough East End constituency. On one occasion the Chancellor of the Exchequer, the late Hon. C. T. Ritchie, had gone down along with Dewar to address the electors. They had a splendid meeting, but at the end of the proceedings the Chancellor found that his overcoat had

been stolen from the ante-room. Mr. Dewar (as
he then was) slipped a sovereign in his agent's
hand and asked him to make an effort with "the
boys" to get back the Chancellor's coat. In about
ten minutes he came back with six coats and sure
enough one of them—not the best either!—was
the Chancellor's. Several nights later Dewar was
back in the constituency when one of his committee-
men came up to him and complained bitterly of
the way he had been treated "in connection with
the lost coat" as he put it.

"Why, I gave a sovereign for its safe return,"
said the whisky king, "wasn't that enough for an
old coat?"

"A sovereign!" shrieked the other. "What a
swindle! I only got a bob from your agent and I
was the bloke that pinched the coat!"

Lord Dewar was fond of telling a story about
myself which has gone round the world "by word
o' mou'," but which I don't think has ever got into
print. It was to the effect that an American tourist
once paid a shilling to inspect the famous old
cottage at Chalfont St. Giles, Buckinghamshire, in
which Milton wrote some of his immortal poetry.
The guide showed his visitor all over the cottage
until he came to the poet's chair and then he
exclaimed dramatically: "In this very chair sat
Milton!"

"Who did you say?" asked the visitor, a look
of disappointment suddenly taking the place of the

keen interest he had been displaying. "Milton? I thought you said Lipton! Give me back my shilling!"

Writing about a great Scotsman like the late Lord Dewar reminds me that I have been on terms of close and intimate friendship for very many years with another Scot whose name is even better known than my own all over the world. I refer to Sir Harry Lauder. Indeed, there were four of us—all Scots—who used to meet very regularly in London—Tom Dewar, Harry Lauder, Andrew Weir (now Lord Inverforth) and myself. We were like brothers. Lord Dewar and Lord Inverforth might be termed the intellectuals of the quartette and it was to them, and particularly the latter, that I used to go when I was in any business quandary or thought I would be the better of some sound advice. Those two men never let me down. And especially of Lord Inverforth I would like to say that I have always regarded him as one of the wisest and shrewdest men I ever met in my life. What he did for Great Britain during and after the War will never thoroughly be appreciated for the simple reason that the public did not know. But the War Cabinets knew and the peerage awarded my splendid friend Andrew Weir was one of the most deserved honours given for magnificent service to the country in her hours of trial.

But to return to Sir Harry Lauder. On every professional visit to London he either lived with me at Osidge, or with our mutual friend "Willie" Blackwood at Harrow. Jocularly he used to say that he got better attention at our houses than he got in any hotel. "And besides," he would add with that little twinkle in his eye, "it's much cheaper!" I don't know what Harry did at Harrow, but at Osidge he simply took command of the house. He was very particular about his meals and ordered just what he wanted at certain specified hours, whether these were the regulation meal hours at Osidge or not. It was very amusing to hear him give his pointed instructions to "John", one of my Cingalese servants.

"At six o'clock, sharp to the second, John, you old rascal, I want ham and eggs, dry toast, and weak tea—without any milk in it! Ham well frizzled and the eggs done on both sides—do you understand? And tell Baker to have the car waiting for me at six-twenty sharp. And that'll be a' the noo, John!" John would stand like a graven image while Sir Harry was giving his instructions and, when the famous little comedian was finished, he would bow solemnly and reply: "Very good, Sir Harry, I got it all here"—pointing to his head. I sometimes thought that John and the other servants were not very sure who was "boss o' the hoose" at such times—Sir Harry Lauder or myself!

Once I played a trick on Harry. Usually he had one of my cars to drive him to and from the London theatres where he was working because, as he himself explained, it was not worth while bringing his own Rolls-Royce from Scotland for a week or two only! So one evening I arranged that instead of the usual limousine one of the factory delivery vans would be waiting for him when he finished his last "show". I made certain that he would refuse to come home in it and hire a taxi. But no, home to Osidge he came in the van! When he arrived I chaffed him about not taking a taxi.

"A taxi from Stratford to New Southgate, Lipton!" he exclaimed. "Why the cost would have been proheebitive!"

The "van incident", however, rankled a bit in Lauder's memory for a long while, but it gave him a chance to cause great laughter among his friends, "for," he said, "the smell of ham which he carried about with him for weeks made all the dogs in the country follow him!"

CHAPTER XIX

*Queen Alexandra's Jubilee dinner—my association
with the Alexandra Trust—I become owner of the
Erin—a boyhood's dream realized.*

IN all likelihood I would have remained very
much less of a public character than I was latterly
destined to become had it not been for two interests.
The first of these was my association with Her
Royal Highness the Princess of Wales (afterwards
Queen Alexandra of much-loved memory) in her
great scheme for providing a dinner to four hundred
thousand of the poorest people in Britain in com-
memoration of the Diamond Jubilee of Her Majesty
Queen Victoria. This wonderful scheme appealed
to my democratic instincts from the moment of its
inception and I threw myself heart and soul into
the task of bringing it to a successful fruition. It
seemed to me that while most of the people in the
country were thinking about military and civic
pageants, the spectacular entertaining of foreign
royalties, ambassadors, and other overseas dignitaries, the Princess had hit upon one of the real big
ideas in connection with the "Jubilee".

Her appeal for funds was not, to say the least
of it, an immediate success. The monied classes
in England—always generous to a degree, let it be

admitted, in subscribing to certain types of charities—did not take kindly to the Dinner Fund for some reason or another, and I was so disappointed at the progress being made that I sent a cheque for £25,000 to the Lord Mayor of London, the custodian of the fund. After this there was never the slightest doubt of the "Poor Folks Royal Dinner" being a successful feature of the festivities.

Naturally being in the catering business I had expert knowledge of what a "banquet" of the magnitude contemplated would call for in the way of organization and supplies and I remember how interested Her Royal Highness was in my calculations of costs and quantities. Each of the guests at this unique feast, which took place simultaneously in all the largest halls in the United Kingdom, was supplied with a meal consisting of meat, bread, plum-pudding, cheese, and cake, apart from tea and coffee and other liquid refreshments. Altogether over seven hundred tons of food were consumed by the Royal "guests". Four hundred vans were employed in the delivery of the meals and ten thousand waiters served them. I doubt if there will ever be such another dinner in the history of the world. I had the honour of going round some of the London halls with her Royal Highness during the progress of the banquet and of saying a few words to the delighted and happy throngs.

A year or two later I again had the great

privilege of working in close association with Her Majesty Queen Alexandra on another project to which she was applying her warm-hearted and generous instincts. This was the establishment of a great popular restaurant in London for the purveying of thoroughly good meals at cost price to poor people. Here, also, I was able to help with practical advice as well as financial assistance. The restaurant was duly founded under the name of the Alexandra Trust. I endowed it with sufficient funds to enable it to carry on its work for all time and I am proud to say that the institution is still to the fore, daily fulfilling its commendable functions and bearing in perpetuity the name of the most gracious and charming lady whose name it bears. For as trifling a sum as one penny it is possible, at the Alexandra Trust, to get a portion of wholesome food while for a few coppers a really good and substantial meal can be obtained. After twenty-five years our cooks and waitresses still serve daily anything from five to ten thousand meals to London's poor people and school-children.

The second of the interests which began to link me more closely with the outer world in the late 'nineties was my passion for yachting. Through the strenuous years of building up my business I had not lost one spark of my early love for the sea. I revelled in my repeated trips to America, for instance, as much for the "whiff of the briny" as for any tangible rewards of my journeyings. The best parts of my holidays were the hours spent upon the water. But it was not until the year 1898 that I found my thoughts definitely and longingly turning again to my boyhood's passion—to the wind and the waves and the salt spray lashing and a mast bending under a well-filled sail. At all events to the actual possession of some craft which would gratify my zest for the sea and give me more frequent respites from the cares of business. The appeal was almost irresistible. And thus it was that I became owner of the *Erin*, the beautiful steam yacht which, in after, happy years, was to be so well-known all over the world.

CHAPTER XX

The Erin *becomes famous for visitors—the Mayor of Boston borrows King Edward's launch—King Edward sees the* Shamrock II *dismasted—the* Britannia *is fitted out to race the first* Shamrock—*the excitement of the trial races—King Edward's fine sense of humour—I get thrown from a horse in a Royal Review in Edinburgh—and complete my convalescence at Balmoral Castle—the Empress Eugenie sails for Ceylon—a rousing reception.*

T HE acquisition of the *Erin* spelt for me a new joy. Only then did I begin to realize that it is not good for any man to be tied, neck and heel, to his office desk. No matter how hard I worked there was always the complete change and pleasure of a week-end on the *Erin* to break the monotony and to give me fresh vitality. Besides, I found I could have much more companionship on my ship than I could possibly have ashore. By and by, the *Erin* became famous for her visitors. Looking back now it gives me intense satisfaction to recall the many prominent and distinguished people to whom I had the honour of acting as host aboard my floating home. And here let me say that these people were not merely aristocrats—they were the men and women who were pulling their weight in the Ship of Life in one form or another.

King Edward himself honoured my yacht and myself with his presence. His Majesty was a lover of the sea and of ships. Queen Alexandra also came aboard to see me as did Princess Beatrice and her daughter, Princess Ena, now Queen of Spain. Indeed, the *Erin's* guest-books contain the names of practically every Royal personage in Europe and of illustrious men and women in every walk of life on both sides of the Atlantic. Yet, I hope to everybody who came on board I was the same, plain Tom Lipton and that I put on no airs and graces when I assumed a yachtsman's cap!

The "informality" which always prevailed upon the *Erin* once led to a rather awkward predicament. American friends were constantly coming to see me on my ship. None were more welcome. Once during Cowes Yachting Week—the chief event of the English sailing season—I was entertaining several Americans when suddenly I observed the Royal launch making direct for my yacht. I took this to mean that Their Majesties the King and Queen were about to pay the *Erin* a visit. At once my American visitors were agog with excitement. The ladies began, anxiously, to practise their formal curtsies, while, in honour of Their Majesties, I ordered my crew to line up to attention. Finally the Royal launch drew up alongside. And who do you suppose jumped out of it? My old friend "Honey Fitz", otherwise Mr. John F. Fitzgerald, the Mayor of Boston, and his two young daughters.

OSIDGE, SIR THOMAS'S PICTURESQUE HOME IN NEW SOUTHGATE, LONDON

You could have knocked us all sideways with a feather, so great was our astonishment and bewilderment.

"My word, Fitz," I exclaimed, "but you have arrived in great style."

"What do you mean?" he asked blankly. "I took the best boat I could see available to bring me over to you." Then he went on to say that, being in London, he had decided to run down for the day and give me a call. Arriving at the sea-front of Cowes he and his family had strolled along to "that building over there", pointing to the sacred steps of the Royal Yacht Squadron, and had "hired the only launch he could see idle at the moment".

It appears he had gone right up to the officer in charge of the Royal Launch and said: "Take us over, please, to Sir Thomas Lipton's yacht," in such a dignified and imperial tone that the officer imagined Mayor Fitzgerald had His Majesty's permission for the use of the launch and promptly did as he was instructed!

But the end of the story is not yet. I learned afterwards that the King and Queen arrived at the steps expecting that their launch would be waiting for them to take them to another yacht on which they had an appointment. It was nowhere to be seen and came back, minutes late, after having carried the Mayor of Boston and his family out to the *Erin*. Fancy the extraordinary situation! The King and Queen waiting impatiently on the jetty while their launch was "hired" by a genial American gentleman to pay a visit to his friend Tom Lipton!

Happily there was a merry sequel to the incident, for, dining with His Majesty on the Royal yacht a night or two later, I had an opportunity of explaining just what had happened. The King was highly amused with the whole story of "Honey Fitz" and his unintentional effrontery and finished up by saying that he would have to cancel the reprimand he had given to his boat's crew for being late!

But it was always King Edward's custom to take a kindly view of any such incident or mishap no matter how serious the personal inconvenience caused to himself. This fine trait in His Majesty's character was strikingly evidenced when, at the time of my second "America" Cup Challenge, the King was on board *Shamrock II* and saw her being dismasted with his own eyes. The mishap was most unfortunate for everybody concerned and peculiarly regrettable in that it took place on the very day King Edward had himself selected to be aboard and sail in one of the trials.

This engagement on the part of His Majesty was one of long standing. For many years he had taken a keen interest in yachting and the performances of his famous cutter *Britannia* were still fresh in the public memory. In making my first challenge for the Cup with *Shamrock* two years previously I had had the gratification of knowing that one of my most sincere well-wishers had been His Majesty. He had even fitted out and raced the *Britannia* against the first *Shamrock* when there was no other yacht which could be tried against my boat. With *Shamrock II,* His Majesty's sympathies were equally manifest but it was a condition of his sailing aboard her that the visit should be entirely informal. Naturally I looked forward with delight to the afternoon's sailing and at luncheon on board the *Erin* we were a most jovial and expectant company. The party included Major General Sir Stanley Clarke, the Royal equerry, the Marchioness of Londonderry (whose interest in my yachting exploits was intense), Mr. and Mrs. Jamieson, and Mr. G. L. Watson, the designer of the challenger.

There was a fair roll of sea on but the brilliant sunshine—typical King's weather—seemed to be the happiest possible augury as, after luncheon, we set out for the challenger and stepped aboard her. The trial race was to be with the original *Shamrock* and the yawl *Sybarita.* The preparatory signal sounded on the *Erin* about two o'clock and four of the five minutes allowed before the actual start had elapsed when the totally unexpected and sensational accident happened to the new challenger. Suddenly, on being rounded up to take a line on the port tack she heeled considerably as she came broadside on to the rather fresh breeze that had sprung up and, without a moment's warning, her whole cloud of canvas swayed and toppled and, with the mast, went over the side.

Fortunately the accident was not so tremendously serious as we all at first imagined it to be. The boom remained intact. His Majesty was standing in the companionway—his favourite position when yachting—and had a view of the accident from first to last. He retained a most wonderful nerve throughout, in this respect being very much calmer than any other person on board. His first inquiry was as to whether anyone had been hurt and he was much relieved to find that all aboard including the first mast-hand had escaped injury. He then lit a cigar and went on smoking calmly until the party could be conveyed back to the *Erin*. Even then the King refused to rest quietly. Knowing how great was my concern that this terrible thing should have happened to my boat while His Majesty was aboard he did his utmost to put me at my ease by assuring me that he was as sorry as I was for the mishap and that it could not have been foreseen by any human being. In fact he insisted on going back in my launch to the *Shamrock* forthwith to view the damage.

We found that the broken mast had doubled under the ship and, touching the bottom, was holding the yacht fast. Meantime it had been necessary to send over to Cowes for rivetters to cut away the mast and so relieve the ship. These men were now busy at the task and His Majesty took as great an interest in their operations as any of the practical yachtsmen in charge.

At dinner on the *Erin* that night, before he went back to London on his special train, King Edward was in as cheery spirits as I have ever seen him. He condoled with me over and over again on my bad luck, did his best to keep everybody in good humour and, when someone remarked that it was curious the boom of the yacht had remained intact, His Majesty wittily remarked:

"Yes, it does seem remarkable for if Sir Thomas's 'boom' did not suffer how are we to account for the bringing down of his 'sales'?"—a palpable joke at my expense which made us all chuckle with merriment.

Actually I never met a man with a keener sense of humour than King Edward. In his informal moments he loved a joke as well as any man that ever lived. Two incidents illustrative of this are recalled to my mind. It so happened that at a Royal Review in Edinburgh at which the King was present, I had—in my capacity as Honorary Colonel of the Sixth Highland Light Infantry—to appear astride a horse. There was nothing very alarming in this prospect so far as I was concerned for I had horses in London and frequently did a good deal of riding. However, a friend in Edinburgh wrote to me saying that there was no call for me to bring north one of my own steeds as he had a very fine horse which he could loan to me for the day.

My friend's idea of a "very good horse" was apparently one that had never been broken in! And on coming to mount the animal just before it was time for my regiment to "march past" His Majesty, I found that the united efforts of four soldiers were necessary to hold it. Immediately I got my feet in the stirrups the wretched beast dashed off with me far ahead of my battalion and careered onwards until we were opposite the grand-stand, on which were seated the King and his nobles and generals and admirals, together with the civic representatives. As if to celebrate my advent under very peculiar circumstances, to say the least of it, fifty massed bands began to blare out at once. This was the last straw. For a few seconds my horse stood stock still, then he turned his head and gave me a most critical stare, examining carefully, it seemed to me, all the decorations on my chest, including the Grand Order bestowed upon me by the King of Italy and other shining medals. Then, deciding that he did not like either me or my decorations, he started to "buck" like an Arizona rodeo-performer. Before I knew it I was fifteen feet up in the air, and when I came down the darned horse wasn't there. Later I woke up in an Edinburgh nursing-home.

A few days later I had an invitation from His Majesty to complete my convalescence as his guest at Balmoral Castle, his beautiful Highland home on Deeside. King Edward was most sympathetic with me over my "accident" at the review, and, after dinner on the night of my arrival, he singled me out from his other guests with the words:

"And now, Lipton, I am going to bestow upon you a new honour!" Saying this he tapped me lightly on the shoulder and added: "I promote you to the Horse Marines!"

Another little story of a great King and a great man. Once His Majesty said to me: "Lipton, I think I shall give you an order shortly."

"This is exceedingly kind of your Majesty," I replied with a twinkle in my eye. "It will do me a lot of good in my business. I shall have a price-list sent to your Majesty at once!" Of course, both of us knew that it was not an order for tea that was being hinted at, but King Edward appreciated my little joke. When shortly afterwards His Majesty gave me this order he did so with a gracious informality which touched me deeply. "Here is a surprise packet for you, Lipton," was all he said. "Please do not open it until you return home." He then handed me a little box which on opening later I found to contain the insignia making me a Knight Commander of the Victorian Order.

But no recollections of the distinguished personages who sailed with me on board the *Erin* would be complete without an allusion to Her Late Majesty the Empress Eugenie. In view of this wonderful old lady's great age—she had then passed her eightieth birthday—no one was more surprised than I was when on motoring down to Farnborough towards the end of 1907 the Empress's secretary, the late Monsieur Pietrie, greeted me with the news: "The Empress would like you to arrange for her to go to Ceylon. You praised the beauties of the island so enthusiastically to Her Majesty when you were last here that nothing will dissuade her from going. She has set her heart on the trip and wants you, as a favour, to make all arrangements as soon as ever you can."

My first instinct was to oppose the trip as being altogether too arduous, although the Empress had travelled with me on more than one long cruise and I knew how hale and hearty she was. A subsequent chat with Her Majesty, however, proving to me that she was very eager to start, I did all in my power to make my venerable old friend's stay in the island as happy and comfortable as possible, and in the early days of January, 1908, I sailed for Colombo, a little in advance of the Royal Party, with that object in view.

Accordingly when a few days after my arrival at Colombo, the P. & O. liner *Mooltan* dropped anchor in the harbour with the Empress and her suite on board, Her Majesty was given a rousing reception, for never in its history had Ceylon been visited by a personage of such historical importance.

I was the first to step on board the vessel to welcome the Empress, and together with the Governor of Ceylon, I accompanied her to the special apartments reserved for the Royal Party in the Galle Face Hotel. Large crowds cheered "the great little old lady", as, dressed in black and heavily-veiled, she made her first progress through the streets of Colombo. The Empress and her party remained for seven weeks on the island and in subsequent years she frequently recalled to me the many happy memories of her trip, which to quote her own words, was "One of the most delightful holidays I have ever spent."

Another interesting memory of Her Majesty is the trip on which I had the honour of accompanying her to Egypt. Her Majesty had expressed to me a desire to revisit the Suez Canal of which, at the height of her power as Empress of the French, she had performed the formal opening in 1859.

You will have observed that I have already made one or two references to the "America's" Cup and my early challenges on behalf of British yachting for that much-prized trophy. Long before I became owner of the *Erin* I had been deeply interested in all the British challenges and in the various representative boats which had left our shores from time to time to sail for the Cup in American waters. Several of the challengers had been built on the Clyde and I followed their fortunes with a tense and fervent hope that they might wrest the famous Cup from the nation which had held it so long and defended it so frequently and keenly.

As a matter of fact the year before I purchased

the *Erin* from Count Florio, her first owner, I had come into the open as a challenger. I issued my "cartel" through the Royal Ulster Yacht Club, the premier yachting body in Ireland. It was accepted by the committee of the New York Yacht Club, headed by Mr. J. P. Morgan, Commodore. These gentlemen met with representatives sent over specially to New York by the Royal Ulster Club and myself, and, after most amicable discussions, a series of matches was fixed up to take place in the late autumn of the following year, 1899. Thus did I enter the lists of "America's" Cup Challengers. That was thirty years ago. I am still in the lists. And more hopeful than ever!

CHAPTER XXI

I issue a challenge for the "America's" Cup—accept-
ance—excitement of preparations—stories of the races
from the beginning—Queen Victoria's interest—I am
determined to lift "that old mug"—breakfast with
Admiral Dewey—Marconi fascinates the world with a
wireless message—my promotion to the New York
Yacht Club—a comedy in coincidence—another chal-
lenge—I take the Erin *to Salonica—work among the*
Serbs—the Erin *is torpedoed and sunk.*

YACHTSMEN everywhere will tell you that the most fascinating story in their ken is the romance of the "America's" Cup. All other tales of the sport of yachting fade into insignificance alongside of that especial and wondrous tale. It has held them in thrall for four-score years. I hope it will continue to do so. Another chapter of the story will be written this year, and once more I am going to have the privilege and honour of helping to write it.

And not only yachtsmen, but landsmen as well, know that the "America's" Cup has come to be regarded as the most-prized trophy—the blue riband—of the yachting world in much the same way as the English Derby has become the greatest prize in the realm of the thoroughbred racehorse. The "America's" Cup! The phrase must have been on everybody's lips for many weeks past. A hundred guinea cup—a piece of silver of the intrinsic value to-day of considerably less than five hundred dollars! That is the actual trophy; surely no fabulous guerdon to be striven for might and main by the finest and most costly racing yachts the world has ever seen! But, as is always the case in true sport, the prize itself means nothing— the winning of it everything. Even the fighting for it is good, healthy, and internationally stimulating.

The story of the "America's" Cup begins eighty years ago with a letter received at the headquarters of the New York Yacht Club from the late Earl of Wilton, Commodore of the Royal Yacht Squadron, then, as now, the premier yacht club of Great Britain. In addressing Commodore Stevens, of the New York Club, the earl wrote as follows:

Sir,

Understanding from Sir H. Bulwer that a few of the members of the New York Yacht Club are building a schooner which it is their intention to bring over to England this summer, I have taken the liberty of writing to you, in your capacity of Commodore, to request you to convey to those members and any friends that may accompany them on board the yacht, an invitation on the part of myself and the members of the Royal Yacht Squadron to become visitors of the clubhouse at Cowes during their stay in England.

For myself I may be permitted to say that

Sir Thomas Among His "Cups"

A UNIQUE PHOTOGRAPH OF SIR THOMAS STANDING BESIDE SOME OF THE HUNDREDS OF TROPHIES HE HAS WON ALL OVER THE WORLD. THE COLLECTION IS PRICELESS IN MANY WAYS AND WAS GUARDED FOR YEARS NIGHT AND DAY BY DETECTIVES

I shall have great pleasure in extending to your countrymen any civility that lies in my power and shall be glad to avail myself of any improvements in shipbuilding that the industry and skill of your nation have enabled you to elaborate.

I remain, sir,
    Your obedient servant,
      WILTON,
Commodore of the Royal Yacht Squadron.

It is clear from this communication that the project of building a yacht to come over to England had already been discussed in America, and it only required the receipt of this friendly letter to clinch the matter. A syndicate of six prominent American gentlemen interested in the sport of yachting was formed and the order given for the construction of the yacht which was to live in history as the *America.*

After some trial races which seem to have been no more than moderately satisfactory she set sail for English waters towards the end of June, 1851. Her sailing powers and her general behaviour at sea encouraged her owners to think that she would perform well against the English yachts.

Those aboard the *America* and her sponsors had certainly nothing to complain of as regards the reception given them on British shores and the hospitality extended to them in every quarter. But when it came to making arrangements for fulfilling the real object of their voyage—a race against an English yacht—there did not seem to be any rush, so to speak, to "accommodate" the American visitor. In almost every way that can be imagined the *America* was a contrast to the purely racing machines that yachts were to become in after years. She was a fine, weatherly vessel, built and rigged to go to sea when it blew a "snorter" as well as in fine winds.

The *America* came in for a good deal of both amateur and professional criticism. It was said that her masts were too heavily raked, her sails too flat, and the impression prevailing among the conservative English yachtsmen of the day seemed to be that she had absolutely no right whatever to move through the water as fast as rumour said she did.

At any rate, whatever the reason, no one seemed inclined to give the *America* a race—and eventually Commodore Stevens posted a notice at the Royal Yacht Squadron headquarters offering to match the schooner against any British vessel for any stake from one to ten thousand guineas.

For some time this offer went begging—though it eventually did lead to one match with the *Titania,* which the *America* won—and the London *Times* newspaper was heavily sarcastic at the expense of the British yachting fraternity, comparing them to a flock of pigeons paralysed with terror at the appearance on the horizon of a sparrow-hawk. However, the "sparrow-hawk" was destined in due course to be put to a test as severe as any that could possibly have been devised.

The Royal Yacht Squadron were to hold a race for a Hundred-Guinea Cup round the Isle of Wight on August 22nd. There were no time allowances, all the squadron boats were eligible to sail, irrespective of tonnage, and a cordial invitation was accorded to *America's* owners to join in.

On the eventful day *America* found herself one of a fleet of eighteen yachts, varying in size from the *Brilliant*—a three-masted schooner of close on four hundred tons—to the *Aurora*, a 47-ton cutter. The size of the *America* is given in the records as 170 tons, so presumably she turned out a rather larger boat than was originally contemplated.

The story of the history-making race can be told in very few words.

One of the last boats to get away, in a light and variable wind, the *America* had worked her way in amongst the leaders by the time the Nab Lightship was reached—a distance of about twelve miles. With the wind freshening, she was soon in the lead. Indeed at one time she held the almost incredible lead of something like eight miles! Towards evening the wind fell light again—lack of wind was the one thing dreaded by Commodore Stevens and the crew of the *America*—but although the *Aurora* managed to close the gap very considerably, the

issue was never in doubt, and the "sparrow-hawk"
from across the Atlantic "got her gun" at 8.34. The
Aurora followed at 8.58 and the third boat nearly
an hour later. Those of the other "pigeons" which
actually finished fluttered home at intervals during
the night!

So it was that what is now known as the
"America's" Cup passed into the hands of Commodore John C. Stevens and was taken back with
him across the Atlantic when he and his friends
returned home.

It is still there in spite of all our efforts to recover
it!

The *America* had become famous in a night.
Queen Victoria, accompanied by the Prince Consort,
visited the yacht the day after her victory. A week
later she sailed her match against the *Titania* over
a course of twenty miles to windward and back—
which she won by just under an hour.

It is not my intention to trace all the Cup Races
from that time down to the present day. Enough
for me to say here that I followed many of the earlier
challenges thrown out by British yachtsmen with
very keen interest indeed. Particularly, I was
roused to enthusiasm by the building on the Clyde
of the challenger *Thistle*. This boat was designed
by my old friend, George L. Watson, who, in later
years, designed *Shamrock II* for me.

The *Thistle* had been eminently successful in her
home waters, winning eleven trophies and three

minor prizes in fifteen races before setting her prow westwards across the Atlantic. And high were the hopes, in bonnie Scotland at least, that at last we had got a chance of retrieving the much-fought-for bit of silver. But once more the defending combination of Edward Burgess, of Boston, and General Charles J. Payne proved too much for the Scottish attacker, and she was beaten pointless.

The challenges issued by the late Lord Dunraven and the matches which took place between his two *Valkyries* and Hereshoff's *Vigilant* and *Defender* in the years 1893-95 will still be fresh in the minds of many yachtsmen on both sides of the Atlantic. From an American angle, they were of distinct interest in that they brought the famous Nathaniel Hereshoff to the fore as a yacht designer. "Nat" Hereshoff was destined to play a very great part for the yachting honour of his country in connection with my own *Shamrock* challenges. And now that I have reached the point of dealing with these, what can I tell you about them that has not already been told?

The first four *Shamrocks* all failed—some less completely than others. But in each one of them my fond hopes were centred. With them I made four attempts to "lift that old mug"—surely the most elusive piece of metal in all the world so far as I am concerned—but I can truthfully say that in the quest of it I have spent some of the happiest hours of my life. Neither money, nor time, nor trouble—aye, nor disappointment—have marred my joy in the pursuit of it. "America's" Cup-hunting has been my principal recreation for over thirty years. It has kept me young, eager, buoyant, and hopeful. It has brought me health and splendid friends.

In the meantime let us glance back ever so briefly over my fortunes with the first four *Shamrocks.*

When I made up my mind to challenge for the world-famous Cup in the summer of 1898, my first intention was to do so with an Irish-built boat out of compliment to my Irish descent and my friends of the Royal Ulster Yacht Club. The hull of the vessel was to be of metal, largely of bronze, and it seemed to me that nobody could carry out work of that character better than the skilled craftsmen of Queen's Island, Belfast, the men who were turning out the best steamships and the fastest liners in the world at that time. But my friend Mr. Pirrie—afterwards Lord Pirrie—the head of Harland and Wolf, dissuaded me from my purpose. Nothing would have delighted him and his firm more, he assured me, than to turn out a challenger for the "America's" Cup, but yacht-building was a specialized art in which it would be folly to allow sentiment to rule. The hull of a racing-boat could be much better constructed, he pointed out, by a firm which had had long experience in the production of speedy light craft, and he suggested I should place the order with some such firm. In the result Thornycrofts were asked to undertake the job. They did so. And the first *Shamrock* was built on the Thames at Millwall.

Mr. William Fife, Junior, designed the first of my *Shamrocks*. When the time came for her to cross the ocean she faced the Atlantic billows bravely, and even when separated from my steam-yacht, the *Erin*, during a storm, her crew were in no way put out, but carried on under shortened sail. By and by she was taken in tow by the *Erin*, and both yachts fetched up safely on the other side after a passage of little more than a fortnight.

My first official reception, forerunner of many such delightful and hospitable receptions at which I have been entertained in America, was given me by a delegation of forty prominent Americans, headed by Colonel George Treadwell, representing Governor Roosevelt of the State of New York. Later the usual gang of Press-boys came aboard, and put me through it in their customary pointed and cheery fashion. The questions an American Pressman won't ask, I always say, would not fill half a page of the smallest notebook on earth! But I enjoy myself in their company immensely. Their ingenuity and inventiveness and good humour and assurance are things to marvel at. They have always been very kind to me.

Soon after the arrival in American waters of the *Shamrock* and the *Erin* an incident occurred on which I delight to look back. I breakfasted with the great Admiral Dewey! It came about in this simple and unexpected manner. We were lying inside the Horseshoe at Sandy Hook when, very early one morning, a big battleship steamed slowly into the bay. At first we could not identify her. We knew that Admiral Dewey was on his way home, but he was not expected for several days. But as the ship came nearer my sailors recognized her as the *Olympia*, the admiral's flagship, from the quarter-deck of which he had directed the United States Navy in their victorious battle with the Spaniards at Manilla. Immediately the news was brought to me I ordered my launch, and, taking with me all the New York papers I could get hold of, I made for the battleship.

Although it was just after daybreak, everybody on board was up and doing. They lowered a gangway for me, and I was soon on the *Olympia* and inquiring after the health of the famous Admiral. As a matter of fact, I was taken at once to his cabin, where I was received with every courtesy, and invited to breakfast. Admiral Dewey was tremendously interested in the forthcoming yacht races, and we had a lot to talk about. On pushing off in my launch an hour later I was astonished to observe large numbers of the crew of the battleship lining the "rails", and holding in their hands packages of a nature which seemed familiar to me. At the same time they were all cheering like mad. At first I was nonplussed at these packages. Then I suddenly remembered that some weeks previously the *Olympia* had called in at Ceylon on her way home from the Philippines, and that I had cabled instructions to my manager out there to present every man of the crew with a package of Lipton's tea. These packages were now on their way home to the sailors' wives and sweethearts!

In connection with my early morning call upon America's great naval hero I am reminded that the "Dewey Reception" celebrations, which took place a few days later, included a magnificent spectacle in which I was privileged to play a part. This was a procession of ships of all kinds—battleships, yachts, tug-boats, ferry-boats; indeed, every sort of craft that floated. In this parade my *Erin* was given the honour of leading the port line, Mr. Pierpont Morgan's *Corsair* doing the same for the starboard section. We sailed slowly and majestically up the Hudson from the Battery to Grant's Tomb. Here we disembarked, and took our places in the land parade by way of Riverside Drive and Fifth Avenue to Madison Square, where had been erected the great Dewey Arch of Welcome and Triumph. That was one of the most interesting days of my life. It concluded by my entertaining in my rooms at the old Fifth Avenue Hotel the two American admirals, Samson and Schley. Not until afterwards did I learn that these distinguished officers were then actually engaged in a very heated controversy, the causes of which I do not even know to this day. But we all had a jolly good meal. Perhaps they settled their differences over "a dram" at my luncheon-table.

But I have wandered from the races. The first bout between *Shamrock* and *Columbia*, the defender, let to no decision, as the time-limit was exceeded. Then a patch of very light, fluky weather succeeding, it was almost a fortnight later before we got enough wind to complete a race. This was won by the American boat. She beat me fairly, squarely, and conclusively. But I could scarcely subscribe to the statement published in one of the New York evening papers that the *Columbia* at one period of the race "shot past Sir Thomas Lipton's challenger like an elevator going past a floor!"

Next day there was more wind, and the *Shamrock* was fully holding her own, when on a hard thrash to windward, her topmast snapped off short. This put us out of action, and we lost the race. October 20th saw the third—and, as it proved, the last of that series of races for the Cup—and again the *Columbia* showed herself to be the better ship in a spanking, whole-sail breeze. She won by just over six minutes. So that ended my first challenge for the "America's" Cup. But I had enjoyed myself so much in America, and had met with such goodwill and kindness, that almost before the "gun" in that final race I had resolved to have "another cut for the Cup".

During the '99 races, of which I have been writing, a young Italian named Marconi demonstrated to an astonished and fascinated world the complete effectiveness of his inventions by sending wireless messages descriptive of the Cup contests to the *New York Herald* and the *Evening Telegram*. This was a magnificent piece of journalistic enterprise which won favourable plaudits all over the world. Mr. Marconi himself took command of the actual work of wirelessing the *Herald* reporter's story from a specially fitted-up broadcasting plant on the steamer *Grand Duchesse*. I always think, in view of what radio has come to mean in our lives to-day, that this was one of the most interesting features of my first yacht racing in American waters.

While the races were proceeding in this and later years, I was fortunate enough to have the pleasure of receiving on board the *Erin* many of America's most famous and distinguished citizens. It would be quite impossible for me to mention them all by name, much as I should like to do so, but it was my pride and joy to have on board with me from time to time men like President Roosevelt, Pierpont Morgan, Mark Twain, Thomas Alva Edison, Henry Ford, and General Nelson A. Miles. There are hundreds of other names in my *Erin* guest-books, and sometimes, when I wish to recall pleasant days and well-loved faces, I take these books up and con through their pages. In addition to the names of my American friends, I find there the signatures of practically every Royal personage in England and Europe, and those of men and women who have

been in the forefront of the social, political, industrial, and progressive movements of the world for
the past thirty years.

Before I returned to England on the completion
of the races against the *Columbia*, I had the honour
of being elected an honorary member of the New
York Yacht Club, a very exceptional compliment,
which I highly appreciated. Other clubs to do me
a similar honour were the Atlantic Yacht Club, the
Larchmont Yacht Club, and the Chicago Yacht
Club. I was also presented by the American people
with a Gold Loving Cup, and this splendid gift is
amongst my most cherished possessions at Osidge,
my London home. In after years I received the
freedom of Chicago and the key of that city, while
the New York Police made me an Honorary Chief,
presenting me with the police flag in Central Park
before a crowd of sixty thousand people. Many
other honours and privileges have been conferred
upon me by my American friends, including
honorary membership of the New York Athletic
Club, the most wonderful organization of its kind in
the world.

The negotiations between the Royal Ulster Yacht
Club and the New York Yacht Club for the 1901
contests were carried through as speedily and
amicably as those of two years before. My second
challenger, *Shamrock II*, was designed by G. L.
Watson, and built at Denny's famous yard on
Clydeside. Everybody associated with her held

SIR THOMAS LIPTON PHOTOGRAPHED ON BOARD THE *ERIN*
ON HIS EIGHTIETH BIRTHDAY

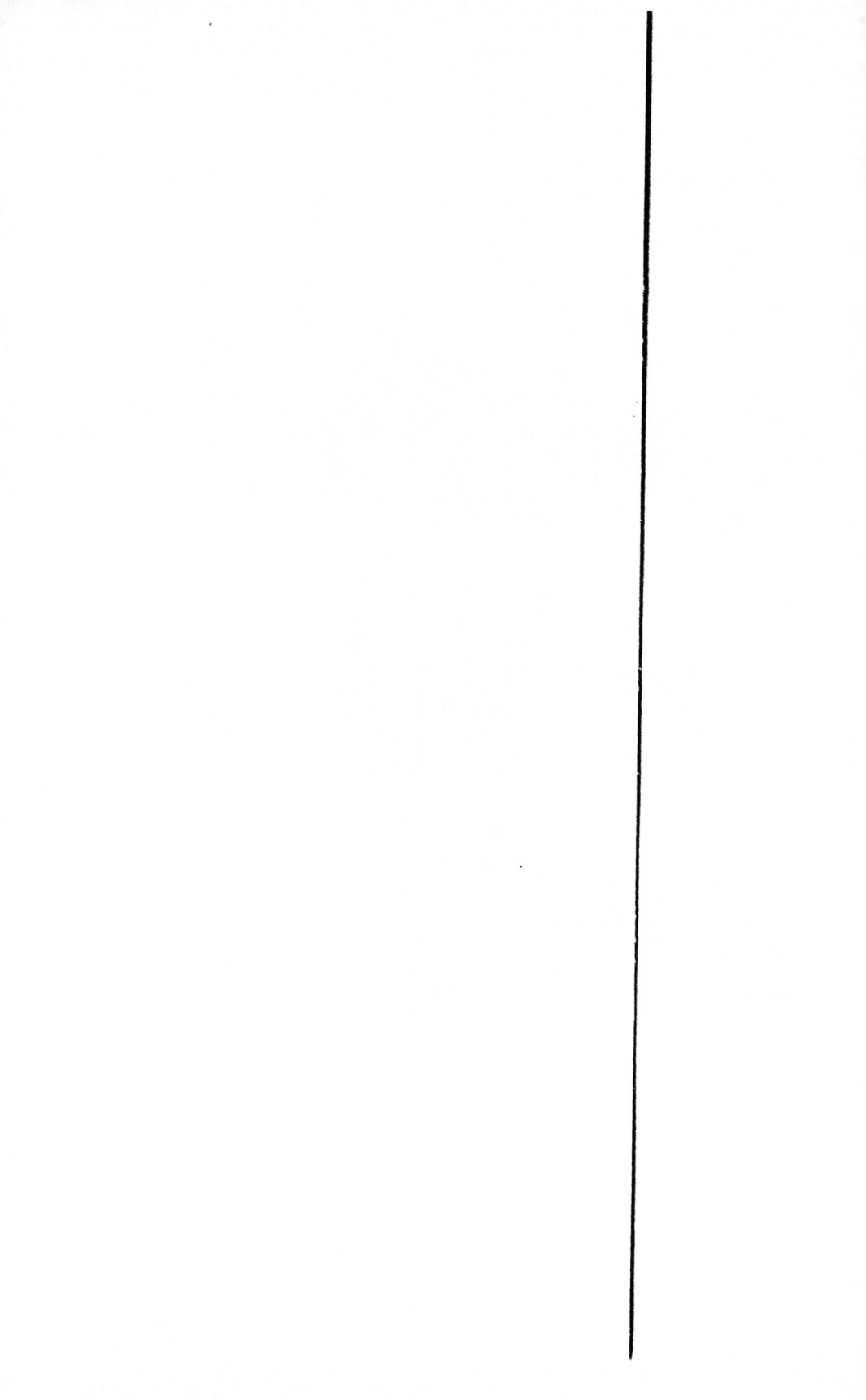

high hopes for her success, but when she came to try her paces against the *Columbia*—again selected to defend the Cup, although other and newer yachts had competed with her for the honour—she was just a shade too slow, for over a series of hard-sailed races my boat lost to the American defender by an aggregate of only three minutes twenty-seven seconds actual time! And this over a total distance of ninety miles—a bit more if the windward work is taken into account! What splendid racing we had that year; I really think that with the slightest shade of luck I might have pulled off a victory. In the last of the series the *Shamrock* crossed the line two seconds ahead of the *Columbia*, but lost because of the time allowance we had to give her. That was a sporting finish, if ever there was one. The British boat was freely admitted to be the best and swiftest challenger ever sent over. But, as Mr. Herbert L. Stone says in his fascinating book describing the races: "The *Columbia* and Charlie Barr were a hard combination to beat!"

Mr. Fife produced in *Shamrock III* an exceedingly beautiful boat, judged by the standards of these days; she was narrower and much longer than her immediate predecessor. Once more we all thought that this time, surely, our turn had come! In her trials with *Shamrock I* in the South of England she performed splendidly. The reason we tried her out with the first *Shamrock* was that the latter was the best boat available, the second challenger being still in America, where I had left her after the races in 1901.

We had not been long in America on this trip when it was borne in on us that, while we had a good ship in *Shamrock III*, the genius of "Nat" Hereshoff had built a bigger and a better one in the *Reliance*. The defender was certainly a "freakish" yacht in many ways, and spread a tremendous amount of canvas—something like sixteen thousand feet, or fully two thousand more than my ship. But that she could travel through the water she demonstrated conclusively by beating *Shamrock III* pointless in all the races of the series. It was not a case of Mr. Fife's yacht being a bad boat, but of Mr. Hereshoff's being a phenomenally good one.

I think that even the Americans themselves were beginning at this time to wish that I might win the precious Cup, and thus let them have an opportunity of showing what they could do with a yacht sent over to our side in the character of challenger. At all events, every time I went over I was the recipient of thousands of mascots; the *Erin's* decks and state-rooms were littered with them. At different times I received no fewer than seventeen Irish terriers; but I had less difficulty with them than with one American eagle which a well-wisher insisted upon my accepting "for luck".

A coloured lady wrote to me saying she had a

son, fifteen years of age, jet black, but with the reddest head of hair in all America. Wherever this unique lad went he took great good luck with him; please, would I take him as a regular mascot? I wrote back explaining that I would be very glad to have the boy, but that I had already a lot of animals on board, and I feared that if I lost the race and let them loose, they would devour the reddest head in all America first!

So far as I know, there is only one man in America who did not view my first three attempts to win the precious Cup with what might be termed an unbiased sporting interest. On the arrival of the third *Shamrock* at Tompkinsville, in New York Harbour, which was always my anchorage point on reaching the American side—this man wrote to me, saying that the windows of his house looked out on the anchorage, that he was happily married to an Irishwoman of the name of Murphy, and that on the occasion of the first *Shamrock's* arrival "opposite their house", his wife celebrated the fact by presenting him with a nice baby boy.

"Things went on all right for us," proceeded the letter, "until your second *Shamrock* arrived. On that very day my wife rose to the occasion with a baby girl. Now your new *Shamrock* has arrived, and the morning she anchored there was another addition to our family—this time another boy. Now, Sir Thomas Lipton, I am not a millionaire. There are over a hundred million people in America, and there is no more loyal citizen among them than I am, but I do hope from the bottom of my heart that you win that darn Cup. But if you don't, on no account come back, or I am a busted man!"

I was so much amused at this letter, which I at first took to be purely a joke, that I sent for the writer. He came—bringing with him his wife and three children. Not only did he bring with him the living evidences of his statements in the letter, he produced the birth certificates of the children, and these actually harmonized with the exact dates of the arrivals of the three *Shamrocks* at Tompkins-ville. I entertained them all on board the *Erin* to the best of my ability, and many a laugh my friends have had over what I still believe to be one of the most extraordinary coincidences that ever came within my direct experience.

My next challenge did not materialize until 1920. Actually all arrangements had been made for a contest between *Shamrock IV* and the American *Resolute* in the autumn of 1914, but it will be remembered that my ship was crossing the Atlantic when war was declared, and the thoughts of all British subjects were turned to much sterner things than international yachting. As a matter of fact, my men aboard *Shamrock IV* and her convoy, the *Erin*, received their first intimation of the declaration of war while they were actually at sea, and a very remarkable circumstance was that they picked up the news by wireless from a German cruiser! The new *Shamrock* was laid up immediately she arrived, and the same course was adopted with the *Resolute*. Nobody associated with the two yachts thought that several years would elapse ere we were to resume our pleasant, care-free fights for the "dear old mug" won by the *America* in the long, long ago. Yet such was to be the case.

As I noted the war-like preparations going on in Britain, and saw the first flower of our young British manhood setting out to fight the enemy, my only feeling was one of regret that I could not put back the years, don the khaki, and march with them to our seaports *en route* for Flanders. As it was, it seemed that the only useful thing I could do was to bring the *Erin* back from America and convert her into a hospital ship for the Allies. I did so, and as early as September, 1914, I was busy conveying parties of doctors, nurses, and orderlies to France under the auspices of the British Red Cross.

A few months later the *Erin* was transferred for service to the Mediterranean. I went with her, of course. Our duty was to carry similar medical parties between Marseilles and Salonica. From the latter base I frequently made journeys by train into the heart of Serbia, where I saw, at first hand, the unspeakable agonies of the typhus epidemic which did such havoc among the allied troops in that country. I also went through many adventures, which, for a man of my age, were rather hair-raising. At Belgrade, for instance, I happened to be caught in the thick of an Austrian bombardment, and how I escaped injury or death I am not very clear to this day.

Working for the Serbs appealed to me, because they were the "little fellows in the big fight". Some such similar reason must have animated the American people, for, long before the United States came officially into the war, they had representatives out in Serbia doing valiant service on their behalf. Indeed, the very first man to come forward when our special Red Cross train drew up at Ghevgeli, the frontier town dividing Serbia from Greece, was the American, Dr. Donnelly, whose heroic self-sacrifice some time later will always remain with me an unforgettable memory.

On the declaration of war Dr. Donnelly had at once relinquished his post as Medical Officer of the Port of New York, and volunteered for work in Serbia. The last time I met him had been in the Lotus Club, New York, some years before, and as we greeted each other delightedly at this wayside station in the far east, neither of us had any idea of how tragic was to be the sequel to our second meeting under such changed circumstances.

The genial and brave doctor explained his presence in Ghevgeli by the fact that he was in charge of two thousand patients, all of whom were lying ill of typhus in a large tobacco factory near the station, and he asked me to come along and inspect his improvised hospital before going further up-country in the Lipton Hospital Train. I agreed to do so, and took with me as many medical comforts as I could spare.

Almost too dreadful to describe were the scenes I saw that day! The bedding accommodation being wholly inadequate, many of the patients had to be placed two, three, and more in one bed. Here and there the dead were stretched alongside the living. Many of the patients were lying on the ground, with straw their only mattress. Dr. Donnelly's difficulties were further increased through the fact that, of the twelve American nurses he had brought with him to this hospital, no fewer than nine had contracted typhus, and he had consequently to rely upon Austrian prisoners for practically the whole of his nursing help. I could not resist the temptation to visit the brave sick nurses, and to talk with them in their miserable quarters. Thoughts of possible infection never occurred to me; it was an honour to mix with young girls of such high courage and lofty devotion to the cause of sick and suffering humanity.

As a prelude to the work which lay ahead of our own Red Cross in Serbia we could hardly have viewed a sorrier scene than that at Ghevgeli, and it was with heavy hearts that we retraced our steps to the little station. Dr. Donnelly and two of his nursing sisters, Miss Tetrault and Miss Fry, took half an hour off from their incessant all-day and all-night toil to see us on our journey. Before bidding me farewell, the doctor explained that Ghevgeli, being near the Bulgarian frontier, was occasionally shelled by the Bulgars, in spite of the fact that the latter had not yet entered the war officially. For the protection, as far as possible, of his hospital, Dr. Donnelly had found it wise to fly an American flag. Unfortunately the only flag he had was a very small one—did I happen to have such a thing on my yacht as a large American Stars and Stripes? I knew, of course, that we had such a flag on the *Erin*, and there and then I telegraphed to my captain at Salonica to have the flag sent up at once. This seemed a very slight service to do for my friend Dr. Donnelly, and I did it gladly, never dreaming, at the time, of the part my American flag would be fated to play in the last chapter of the gallant doctor's life-story!

Two or three weeks later, when my first relief expedition to Serbia was drawing to a close, I wired to the doctor, stating the hour my train would be passing through Ghevgeli on its way to the coast, and expressing the hope that he and the same nurses who had seen me off would again be at the station to give me a handshake, and let me know how they were faring. But when the train reached Ghevgeli there were no nurses—and no Dr. Donnelly. My heart sank within me as I looked eagerly in every direction for the brave souls I had been expecting to see. I had a premonition of tragedy. Why, I know not. But my worst fears were realized when

Dr. Hodge, an assistant doctor from the hospital, stepped forward and said:

"We had your telegram, Sir Thomas, but Sisters Tetrault and Fry are down with typhus. And Dr. Donnelly——"

He turned away for a moment, and then added: "Dr. Donnelly died of typhus yesterday, Sir Thomas."

Nothing more was said between us at the time. We could only stand on the station platform and grip each other's hands.

Later Dr. Hodge told me how Donnelly, when seized with the dread illness, dictated nine letters, including one for his wife in the United States. He said that if he recovered he would look after the letters himself, but if he died they were to be given to me for dispatch to his friends. And just before he died Dr. Donnelly left one more instruction. His last request was that his body might be wrapped in the American flag sent up from the *Erin*, and that the dear emblem of his country should be consigned to the grave with his remains.

Needless to add, I carried out my departed friend's instructions with regard to the letters, and on a second visit to Ghevgeli later in the same year I had a special photograph taken of the doctor's grave, at the head of which a large stone cross had been erected. This picture I sent to the sorrowing widow in America, and just how grateful this lady felt for the courtesy was shown four years later, in

March, 1919, when I paid my first visit to New York after the war. To my great surprise the first two people to greet me as I disembarked from the *Aquitania* were Mrs. Donnelly and her bonny six-year-old laddie, who had come down specially to the Cunard Wharf to thank me. I was exceedingly touched.

I have told you this story of a noble American gentleman who sacrificed his life in the Great War, far from home and kindred, because it made a very powerful impression on me. But many fine American doctors, such as Dr. Donnelly, and many women like Sisters Tetrault and Fry, came over to Britain from America during those awful years and took up dangerous posts along with our own British doctors and nurses. I met them everywhere in Europe, big-hearted men and women, with everything to lose and nothing to gain, and all of them setting examples of heroism and devotion to ideals which inspired everybody with whom they came in contact.

For so long as, from the standpoint of the Allies, there remained a Serbia to go to, my ship continued to ply between Marseilles and Salonica. I came to love the brave Serbs. I was happy amongst them. And they were altogether too grateful to me for any work I was able to perform on their behalf. They conferred upon me the freedom of the City of Nish, then their temporary capital, a distinction given to no other foreigner. The present King of Serbia also

SIR THOMAS LIPTON FEEDING ONE OF THE LITTLE GIRL
PASSENGERS ON BOARD THE *CEDRIC* WITH GRAPES

created me a Knight of the Grand Order of St. Sava, and this decoration I am proud of, and it constantly reminds me of intensely interesting times spent in the country of the Serbs. The Serbian people called me Chica Toma—Uncle Tom—and for many months that was my only appellation among them.

At length, when the enemy invasion of Serbia rendered my work there impossible, I returned to take part in other war duties in England. But the *Erin* remained in the Mediterranean as a patrol ship under the British Admiralty, and it was while she was engaged in this duty that she was torpedoed by a submarine. My beautiful and historic yacht went to the bottom of the sea, carrying with her, alas! six members of my crew. For the life of any one of these I would gladly have given the ship.

The challenge with *Shamrock IV* was deferred for exactly six years. Yachtsmen on both sides of the ocean were naturally keen to renew their friendly contests, and when I went over shortly after the finish of the war, I was given one of the greatest receptions of my life. Once more, as always happens to me when I am accorded these princely greetings on arriving in New York, my thoughts flew back to the far-off day, over sixty years ago, when I stepped ashore at the Battery as an emigrant lad with less than thirty shillings in my pocket. And I can never help at such moments contrasting the luxury of living in a first-class hotel with my experiences in Mike McCauligan's boarding-house, where at mealtimes, unless you ate quick and had a long arm, you got devil a bite to eat!

Immediately I landed my first concern was to see my challenger, and on going to City Island, where she had been laid up during the war years, I was delighted to find her little the worse for her long period of masterly inactivity. In the actual races of 1920 we did better than we had ever done before. Of the five races sailed I won two. One of these victories was due, it is true, to an unfortunate mishap to the defender, which I regretted as much as my opponents. Moreover, when the *Resolute* recorded the first of her three victories, the margin by which she won was no more than the time my ship had to allow her under the then existing measurement rule. So far as pure sailing was concerned, it was virtually a dead-heat. And in one at least of the defender's two other victories rather baffling weather seemed to like us less than it did our opponent. But I did not grumble. It is all in the game. We had had a series of splendid races, and I had, at any rate, the melancholy satisfaction of knowing that in the final result the better boat had won.

Now my challenge with *Shamrock V* is within appreciable distance of being fought out. As all the world knows, this year's races will be sailed under considerably different conditions from those in former years. Not only will both challenger and defender have been built to the same Universal Rule, but in the construction of the yachts the requirements of Lloyd's Register rules for yachts will have been fully complied with. The new rules will ensure that both yachts are not extreme examples of types, and that, broadly speaking, they will be fit for general service *as* yachts, and not useless for everything else but racing. In my humble opinion this is a most happy outcome of the negotiations that have taken place from time to time, and always in the most friendly and genial spirit, since I became a challenger for the famous trophy. One pleasant result of the change will be that public interest is likely to be keener than ever in international yachting, and, indeed, in all branches of yachting. The development is one which was bound to come, and, having come, it will be welcomed everywhere.

This summer I have spent many weeks on board my new steamship *Erin*—yes, I have now another and a larger *Erin*—and it has been my joy to see my *Shamrock V* win many magnificent races all round the British coast against the best of the yachts on our side of the water. What, then, of my very latest challenger? I can truthfully say that Mr. Nicholson has turned out a fine boat, and one that has, as I have just mentioned, given evidence of being a fast mover under varying conditions. Her skipper is Edward Heard, of Tollesbury, and we are all hopeful that the struggle will see him at the top of his form. With my old friend and trusty yachting advisor, Colonel Duncan Neil, to lend him the benefit of his shrewd and lengthy experience, I am more than hopeful that Captain Heard will distinguish himself.

Of Duncan Neil I would like to say this—he is one of the truest-hearted Scots it has ever been my good fortune to be associated with. He and I have been shipmates and "cronies" for a very long number of years. He has been my guide, philosopher, and friend in all my yachting challenges and adventures and, in addition, my delightful colleague and friend in many trips to different parts of the world. I always say that if I have one regret at all in connection with my *Shamrocks*, it is that I never have had one quite good enough to win the "America's" Cup; had I possessed one, Duncan Neil would have sailed her to victory with skill equal to that of the best yachtsman who ever trod a deck or squinted aloft at the lie of a sail in a stiffening breeze. Quiet, honest, straightforward, and manly in all things and in every way, Duncan Neil has meant a great deal to me in my full and extended life.

Now I must, like the Scottish ministers, draw my discourse to a close. To be perfectly honest about the matter, I have only consented to relate these impressions and recollections because I have been urged to do so by many dear and valued friends. To say that I dislike publicity would come rather badly from a man who has used publicity for his business affairs to an extent few merchants in the world have equalled! Yet the fact remains that so far as my own private life is concerned, I certainly have never been anxious to write or speak about it. And I have only done so in this volume for two reasons—one, that my British friends assured me it would give them pleasure to have some sort of record of my life and, two, so that I could take the opportunity, here and there in my memoirs, of showing my love and respect for that great country across the seas to which I have been a constant visitor for more than sixty years.

I refer, of course, to the United States—that vast, vivid, thrustful family of peoples drawn from all the corners of the earth and now happily welded together in the bonds of a great national pride and in the knowledge of stupendous accomplishments achieved and yet to be achieved. I always say that you have to live in America, as I have done, boy and man, thoroughly to know and appreciate the people just as we in Britain are only known and truly appreciated by those Americans who are continually coming amongst us. And if, during all the years that have gone since I first set foot on American soil, I have been helpful in the smallest degree in cementing the relationship between my own land and the citizens of the United States—well, I have had the gratification of seeing my fond desires become more and more realized. The differences between us are only superficial; the fundamentals are the same, in outlook and aspiration, in character and ideals.

CHAPTER XXII

The arts of salesmanship and its relation to the other kind of sailsmanship—my creed of success in business.

I DO not think I could conclude my book on a better note than to give a fatherly word or two of advice from a very old man, who has worked tremendously hard all his life, to those at the threshold of their careers. And this advice, while it is my own in idea and substance, was thrown into proper shape for me many years ago by my principal private secretary, Mr. John Westwood, a faithful, brainy, cultured Scotsman who has been at my right hand every hour and every day for something like thirty years. I had been asked to attend a conference on "Salesmanship", but I found I could not "make the date", so I asked Mr. Westwood to draft out something on lines I roughly indicated to him. And this is what we produced together as a message from Tom Lipton to be read at the conference:

"The subject of salesmanship has been one of very special interest to me all through my business life. I suppose I can claim to be something of a salesman; anyhow, I have been selling both personally and by deputy since I was a youth, and in my early days I was supposed to be not without gifts as a salesman. I have also had some little experience of the other kind of sailsmanship—that with which my *Shamrocks* are more particularly identified—and while at first sight it may not seem that there is much in common between the two, it will be found, on examination, that they are more or less related. To begin with, both depend to a large extent on atmosphere and air, or rather wind; in the one case 'hot air' is said to be occasionally utilized!

"The ideal conditions for the sailsman on the water are a sunny atmosphere and a strong, true, and steady breeze, and for the salesman of commerce a sunny and cheerful mental atmosphere and a strong, reliable, and attractive line of goods. They must both be sportsmen at heart, ready and prepared to take the bad weather with the good, depression and squalls equally with prosperity and fair winds, and both must play the game squarely and honestly. The salesman of commerce using other than straightforward methods may get the weather of his customer once and land him with a 'dud' deal or 'soak' him in the matter of price, but he dare not show his face in that quarter again. The only man who can do this with anything like impunity is the one whose territory is big enough to make his one round last a lifetime!

"So must the sailsman give way cheerfully when caught on the wrong tack, and at all times respect the rule of the road. Just as the sailsman must keep a constant look out for changes of weather, so must the salesman keep his eyes skinned for changes of taste; as the one watches for puffs of wind, the other must watch for freaks of fashion; as the one when he gets into the doldrums puts up his helm and goes off to look for a favouring breeze, so must the other in times of slackness break new ground and hustle for fresh business. Then, if the winds are contrary, the sailsman must tack (t-a-c-k) to make progress and coax his boat over the winning-line just as the salesman must use tact (t-a-c-t) to overcome the obstacles he may meet with and coax his customer into giving him the coveted order and thus make his the winning line.

"The first essential of success as a salesman is to make sure that he has a good article to sell, as, unless he has faith in his own line, he can hardly hope to persuade or enthuse his customer, and, having that faith, he should endeavour to impart it to those whose business he is out to get. He should also make himself well-acquainted with the article he is selling, so that he can talk about it as an expert if necessary. He should also make equally sure that his goods are what his customers require; it is no use trying to force an article nobody wants, and if he has not got the right goods to sell, he should report accordingly to his house, giving them the exact particulars of what is wanted and urging them to manufacture the thing that will go.

"Much of the success in the commercial world of

SIR THOMAS LIPTON GREETS HIS OLD FRIEND SIR HARRY LAUDER
IN NEW YORK

a nation is due to the alert ability of its representatives in finding out what merchants all over the globe are wanting and setting themselves to produce the right article.

"Another point I would suggest is—don't belittle your opponents' goods. Admit their merit (if they have any), but tactfully point out the advantages of your own and show in what way they are superior. Again, don't take offence readily. You may not always be received with open arms by your customer. Don't expect the fatted calf to be killed for you every time you call. Make allowances for the customer. You don't know his troubles or annoyances—he may have lost his collar-stud or be wearing a pair of tight boots! Try to give the soft answer that turneth away wrath and he will probably decide that he has done you an injustice and will strive to make amends to your ultimate advantage.

"Above all things be civil, polite, and conciliatory. Whatever the station of life your customer may be in, whether he is proprietor, or manager, or head of a department, or only the owner of a one-horse show in a small village, make him feel that for you he is the one man in the universe and that to obtain his order is the ambition of your life. Get close to your man; win his confidence and, having got it, make sure you keep it. It was my aim in my own early days in serving as many customers personally as I could to make each of them my friend, and I am proud to say that I mostly succeeded; indeed, I frequently receive reminders from some of these good people that they knew me when I was behind the counter.

"In exactly the same way that the sailsman afloat should keep his craft trim and neat, his brasses burnished bright, and his sails spotlessly clean, so should the salesman ashore be spruce and smart in his personal appearance—preserving at all times his own self-respect and the credit of his house, and justifying to the full his claim to the title and position of 'an Ambassador of Commerce'."

A LOVABLE
AND UNIQUE PERSONALITY
by
WILLIAM BLACKWOOD

WHEN Sir Thomas and I completed the life-story told in the foregoing pages he was within a few weeks of sailing for New York to see his *Shamrock V* make her unavailing bid for the great prize to the winning of which he had devoted so many years of his life and an aggregate sum of money not far short of a quarter of a million pounds sterling. He was fairly confident that at last, chiefly on account of the change in the rules governing the "America's" Cup contests, he stood an excellent chance of achieving his life's ambition.

Yet no more confident than on other occasions. Confidence and optimism, indeed, were his perpetual and unfailing characteristics. I saw him off to America in the late summer. He stepped along the platform at Waterloo Station with all his old jauntiness; the blue reefer suit was as trim and tailor-like as of yore and the blue-spotted tie as prominent as ever beneath the peaked collar. He had his usual jokes for everybody. I, who had known him for fully twenty years, was amazed at

269

his freshness and vitality and I could not help whispering to John Westwood—the finest secretary any great man was ever blessed with; loyal, painstaking, ubiquitous, suave where suavity was the correct note and unbending if it were a case of serving his master's interests—that "the old man would still be the same ten years hence!" But Westwood shook his head. He realized that Lipton's wonderful physique was on the wane even while his indomitable spirit remained unassailable. "Sir Thomas is making his last trip across the Atlantic!" he quietly said in my ear. And these words proved true.

The defeat of *Shamrock V* he accepted with his customary smiling fortitude. But when he came to make his speech at the frantically-enthusiastic reception given him in New York a week or two after the races he faltered for the first time in his life and had to sit down in the middle of it. Friends of my own who were with him on that occasion were fearful that the ceremony might have a tragic ending. Yet he recovered amazingly. His return to Osidge saw him improve greatly in health. I dined with him several times within the past few months, and I must frankly say that I never in my life saw a man of eighty-one so sprightly, so rudely healthy-looking, or one who took a greater interest in his food.

Incidentally the meals at Osidge were always the same—soup, fish, meat or chicken and rice-pudding and fruit. He partook of each course and generally finished with a decidedly liberal helping of fruit. When I told him—as I always did—that the grapes from the Osidge hot-houses were the finest in the world he was immensely pleased and insisted upon heaping my plate with far more of the luscious fruit than I could hope to consume. Sir Thomas ate rice at least twice every day of his life. It was cooked in the Ceylon method by "John", the elder of the two Cingalese servants, and practically every guest was told by Sir Thomas that "John's rice-puddings were the best in Britain!" Indeed, that faithful and devoted henchman had very often to write out the recipe so that visitors could take it away with them and thus be in a position to have rice served at their own tables in the "Lipton fashion". Those diners at his table who commended his rice dishes were very popular with the old gentleman!

Actually Sir Thomas was deeply immersed in a still further challenge for the "America's" Cup right up till the end. He was determined to have another "cut for that Cup", as he phrased it, and when he and Duncan Neil, his yachting mentor and close associate in all the challenges, came down to discussing details the old man's eyes would light up with enthusiasm; there was little of the octogenarian about him on these occasions! I think that at heart he was exceedingly pleased at his election to membership of the famous Royal Yacht Squadron—the most exclusive club in the universe, as it had been described—in the evening of his days, but had the honour, ungraciously withheld for so many years, come earlier in his yachting career he would have appreciated it much more. Last summer he was racing with the *Shamrock* in the Solent during Cowes Week, but not once did he set foot in the Royal Clubhouse. And many of his friends secretly rejoiced thereat!

Naturally, I did not know Sir Thomas, in his Glasgow business days or even in the early years of his firm in London for he was a world-famous character while I was still at school. But I have met many of his colleagues of those times and I never became wearied of their stories of his amazing energy, resource, adroitness and determination to build up a business the like of which no single man has ever been responsible for in the history of shop-keeping. In his own times and in his own trade he was absolutely unique. Everything he tried he made a success of. And he was not satisfied merely with success—it had to be colossal success. He reckoned nothing a triumph unless he had achieved the almost unbelievable, the unattainable! And for forty years and more he worked like a galley-slave, not because he had to but because he loved working. One minute he would be signing cheques for enormous sums of money in payment of gigantic business deals or for Inland Revenue charges, the next he would be giving a few encouraging words to the latest message-boy in his employment, and probably the following morning he would be behind the counter of a new shop, white-jacketed-and-aproned, selling the first pound of ham or butter to an Aberdeen or a Portsmouth or a Dublin house-wife!

To be quite candid, the vastness of the organiza-tion he had built up became, latterly, too much for his single-handed capacities. If Lipton had a fault in business—especially in a business of such world-wide ramifications as he had established—it was that he did not trust the control very far away from his own hands. While he was young and virile this did not matter so much, but when, ten or a dozen years ago, he had to face very able and strenuous competition, his "dourness" (the best word I can find to describe a characteristic which became pro-nounced as he grew older) led to results in the organization not altogether satisfactory from a shareholder's standpoint. Lipton was loth to realize that at seventy, say, he was not so fitted to manage a huge concern as he was at forty. Again, he could not be brought to understand that businesses had to move with the times—even an amazing business like Lipton's Markets. Latterly he was prevailed upon to retire, but he did so with a very unwilling heart. His pride was hurt; he could not imagine a world for him, and a life for him, which did not include going down to the great City Road headquarters every morning at nine o'clock! The last occasion I visited him in his office in London I shall never forget. He was like a child from whom a beloved toy had been taken roughly and cruelly. He did not realize that what had been done was done in his own best interests. He was full of pathetic regrets and rather stupid resentments against his most faithful friends. As I said farewell to him, trying to hold out a rosy vision of many years of peaceful enjoyment at Osidge and on his lovely yachts, I saw a tear in Tom Lipton's eye.

There never lived a more simple man than the Lipton I knew. Outwardly simple, that is. He had little or no "learning", as the world understands the word; science, politics, the arts interested him not at all. I never heard him discuss the daily events of the hemispheres as they were reported in the newspapers. Try to draw him into a conversation on any one of the hundred topics the ordinary man takes delight in discussing, be it never so superficially, and Lipton would listen for a few minutes. Then suddenly he would veer right away and come out with some completely inconsequential remark about himself, his business acumen, his yacht, or one or other of the Royal personages he had had the honour of entertaining! It was quite enough for him that he was Tom Lipton, that he was known to everybody and respected by all, that he owned the best yacht on the seas, and that his "log-books" contained the signatures of the best people on earth.

He was the most self-centred and self-sufficient individual I have ever met in my life.

Yet with it all he put on no airs whatever; his geniality (unless in very special circumstances) never failed to radiate all round and about him. Yes, he was very simple. But let anybody attempt to "put one over on him", let a visitor try to probe into matters which were none of his concern, let fawners and favour-seekers subtly work their guile upon him, let friends (as I have heard them) jocularly endeavour to know what he was going to do with all his wealth after he had no further use for it—Sir Thomas was not so simple then! No, on such occasions he was a very shrewd old bird with a knowing eye for the net and the lime. I never caught him napping—and I knew him as well as most of his narrow circle of really intimate friends!

The world has lost a great character in Sir Thomas Lipton. Starting life with no advantages, save the fine influence of a mother whom he worshipped and to whose advice he listened carefully throughout her life, he carved his way to the extreme forefront of the world's commerce, became the friend and confidant of Royalty, and achieved for himself in the realm of international sport a name which will live for all time. It is inconceivable to me that there can ever be such another as Tom Lipton. He made his own standards; his defects were, to a great extent, his peculiar qualities; he was absolutely unique in everything that he did, said, and thought.

INDEX

INDEX

CPSIA information can be obtained at www.ICGtesting.com
Printed in the USA
BVOW11s0010291015

424699BV00020B/229/P